D0482329

DISCARD

Cold Feet

BF
619
R48
1988

IRVINE VALLEY COLLEGE LIBRARY
SADDLEBACK COMMUNITY COLLEGE DISTRICT

17899

Cold Feet

Why Men Don't Commit

DR. SONYA RHODES AND
DR. MARLIN S. POTASH

DISCARD

E. P. DUTTON NEW YORK

Copyright © 1988 by Dr. Sonya Rhodes and Dr. Marlin S. Potash
All rights reserved. Printed in the U.S.A.

No part of this publication may be reproduced or transmitted in any form
or by any means, electronic or mechanical, including photocopy, recording,
or any information storage and retrieval system now known or to be
invented, without permission in writing from the publisher, except by a
reviewer who wishes to quote brief passages in connection with a review
written for inclusion in a magazine, newspaper, or broadcast.

Published in the United States by E. P. Dutton,
a division of NAL Penguin Inc.,
2 Park Avenue, New York, N.Y. 10016.

Published simultaneously in Canada by
Fitzhenry and Whiteside, Limited, Toronto.

Library of Congress Cataloging-in-Publication Data

Rhodes, Sonya.
Cold feet.

Bibliography: p.
1. Commitment (Psychology) 2. Intimacy (Psychology)
3. Men—Psychology. 4. Love—Psychological aspects.
5. Single people—Psychology. I. Potash, Marlin S.
II. Title.
BF619.R48   1988   155.3′32   87–27150
ISBN 0–525–24634–7

DESIGNED BY EARL TIDWELL

3 5 7 9 10 8 6 4 2

To our husbands

Contents

Contents

Acknowledgments

We want to thank Susan Schneider whose untiring devotion and editorial talents made an outstanding contribution to this project. We couldn't have done this book without her.

We are also indebted to all the men and women who shared their lives with us. Their contribution is on every page. We also owe special thanks to Geri Thoma who was always there when we needed her.

My dear friend, Jean Marzollo, once again generously gave her time and patience. I especially value her professional review and criticism at various stages of the project.

Particularly helpful in discussing concepts and reviewing drafts of the manuscript were Monica Halpert, Barbara Kass, Ann Jackler, Vinton Taylor, Ceil Weissman, and Nancy Wolff. I am also indebted to Jon Banton, Stephen Dickstein, Rene Goldmuntz, Lisa Rothblum, and Steven Dreyfus for offering their time and wisdom, and to Alan Alper who found a special way to be included in this book.

My husband, Bob, gave support, opinions, and (lest I forget) the male point of view at every stage along the way and, as my best friend and trusted advisor, I am thankful. My son, Justin, and my daughter, Jennifer, made me aware on a daily basis of how male and female relationships are defined in the minutia of a New York City school. As teenagers, they are unknowingly struggling with the issues described in this book, and have fueled my belief in this project.

SONYA RHODES

September 1987

I owe my gratitude to all my patients throughout the years for trusting me to visit their inner lives. The experiences they have shared with me have been central in helping me to formulate the ideas for this book. My thanks to those who have participated in my courses and workshops, and to my professional colleagues in psychotherapy, business, and teaching. I thrive on our provocative conversations and the new questions they continually raise.

To Barbara Potash and Henry Druker, my deepest appreciation for the time and energy spent assisting in the interview process.

To my parents, who taught me about commitment and who have maintained their commitment to each other for forty-five years, I will always be thankful. My wonderful husband Fred helps me understand the effort and rewards that go into living commitment on a daily basis. To my daughter Laura, who makes commitment a joy, and my daughter Hilary, who waited patiently until this book was complete, thankfulness beyond words.

MARLIN S. POTASH

September 1987

Why We Wrote This Book

Today's women are the first in history to achieve sexual liberation, financial independence, and professional success. They should be happier and more fulfilled—professionally and personally—than any other women before them. Are they? No. Over the last five years, we've noticed a new phenomenon in our psychotherapy practices and clinical research: women who *should* be happy are asking instead why their relationships with men are failing.

The stories from women clients pour in. "I'm thirty-two and I want to have a family. I've lived with my boyfriend for three years, but he freezes when I talk about marriage. He says he has to keep his options open." "My boyfriend doesn't have a problem with the 'M'-word—after two years of casual dating, we don't even have a relationship yet!" "I've been seeing the same man for a year—why does he turn off sexually whenever we seem to be getting close?" "I met a man last night, and it was *electric*—an instant go. He seemed to be really interested in me and seemed to understand that I didn't want to go to bed on the first date. How come he never called me back?"

The men we see in our practices (more now than ever before) are in pain, suffering from discomfort, unease, and a downright terror of intimacy that we've never seen before. The symptoms are psychic chills and trembling at the *very idea* of closeness with a woman. We call it the Cold Feet Syndrome, and it is an epidemic. Every man in our society suffers from it, at least to some degree. We won't pull any punches. Not only are men different from us, but they are amateurs at intimacy. Men in our society have not been trained to be intimate—and for the first time in history, commitment means emotional connection, not financial responsibility.

The news isn't all bad. Some men today are more sensitive and more truly desirous of intimacy than their fathers were. But even though a man may want a woman, not a wimp, he may also be put off and frozen out by the demands she places on him. With 1980s women, men are at once scared and enticed, put off and turned on, abhoring and adoring. Men are overwhelmed by women's demands at the same time that they are thoroughly attracted to women who are strong, sexy, and outspoken about their needs and expectations. At this emotional crossroads—where he is torn between dread and desire—a man experiences cold feet.

Meanwhile, women who should be happy are asking: "Am I doing something wrong? Am I to blame?" Nothing could be further from the truth!

But if you glance at even a few of the current popular books on male/female relationships, you'll be told that men are pretty much okay (except for a few minor quirks), while women (who just can't be happy) are driven to self-destruction. The assumption is that women, woefully misguided at best, wildly neurotic or willfully wrongheaded at worst, bear the full burden of blame for relationship breakdown. Reading these books—and taking them as gospel—would leave any normal, healthy woman wondering if she were a candidate for the couch. In our practices, workshops, and lectures, we've seen sane women struggling to unearth pathologies that don't exist! "Another relationship down the tubes . . . my therapist tells me I'm attracted to rotten guys, and that I have to work on it." "How come I make good decisions at the office, but when it comes to my personal life, I always louse things up? Something must be wrong with me." And on and on.

Your therapist, your friends, or your mother may "analyze" you to death, telling you that you set yourself up to fail, or that you're "scared" of commitment. This isn't true. Most women move easily and naturally into intimate relationships—when men are available for intimacy. Women work hard at commitment. Women *want* commitment. From our work with men we know that you are having problems in relationships because *men* cannot commit.

"It's anti-male," one woman argued while we were discussing our findings and conclusions. "Instead of blaming women, you're blaming men. What's the point?"

Are we blaming men? No. In this book *no one* takes the rap. But if you hear a loud crash, it's the sound of taboos breaking as we focus on men's problems instead of women's. Initially, you may dislike this idea—many women do. As women, all of us have been raised and trained to protect men; if there is a problem in a relationship, we prefer to think it is *our* problem. Then, we can spend night and day toiling in the vineyards of the relationship, trying to "work it out."

For ourselves and for the women we work with, going beyond the last great taboo is an ongoing process—and often a painful one. So, as you read this book, we know you'll have a strong, gut reaction to it. The women we have worked with typically go through several stages:

1. Resistance: "Men are okay; I'm the one who's screwed up."
2. Fear: "If men are so screwed up, does this mean I'll never have a relationship?"
3. Blame: "All men are awful. Everything is their fault, and it's hopeless."

4. Acceptance: "Okay, it's tough, but it's real. How should I deal with it?"

By the time you "accept" the new reality, you'll feel pure relief at knowing that it isn't your bad luck or bad choices that are causing all the problems. It's freeing when you begin to understand that the problem lies outside yourself. And the news gets even better: Men's problems with commitment *can* be resolved (once you and he recognize them).

In the 1980s, commitment has a new definition. Both partners do the emotional and physical "chores" of a relationship, sharing their emotional lives and coping openly with issues of power and control, sexual and otherwise. Neither partner is assumed to be in charge, nor does one or the other take care of the relationship. Both partners do, and both benefit from a new kind of closeness.

Today's women and men are capable of carving out a new kind of intimacy—once women know what they're up against and men are willing to take on the challenge. "Why do men hold back?" one woman asked. "Are they lazy?" Sometimes. But it's really more than that. Often it's just plain, brute fear. Once a man opens himself to a woman, he has opened a Pandora's Box of vulnerabilities—he fears that he will no longer be in control of himself, of her, of anything. He may be exposed as inadequate or irrational. Also, he's never had to do it before. What men don't understand—and women do—is that the pain is more than worth it. When your reward is closeness—true intimacy—the blood, sweat, and tears pay for themselves.

Among the major questions we will answer are:

1. Why is commitment-phobia an epidemic today?
2. What are men really afraid of?
3. What are the first signs of a man on the run?
4. What is the profile of the guy who is a bad risk for commitment?
5. How can you tell a good bet from a bad one?

6. Why is the most desirable woman also the most threatening?

7. Why are women better at intimacy than men?

8. How do men disguise their commitment problems?

9. What does it mean when a man turns off sexually, and when is his sexual behavior a sure sign of a commitment problem?

10. Why has "commitment" become a dirty word to men?

11. Do all men have cold feet—or does it just seem that way?

As we answer these questions, we'll define the three types of men with cold feet and outline the Five Levels of Commitment so that you know where you stand. We'll equip you with techniques to deal with commitment stalemates, and tell you how commitment problems are disguised in sexual behavior. We'll also discuss what happens when you're ready for a child and he isn't, and commitment problems in marriage. Finally, we're including a special chapter, "For Men Only," that you can tear out and show to your lover that will help him realize what he is doing in the relationship.

We are two psychotherapists in private practice in New York City. Our research is documented by extensive clinical work with couples, workshops, seminars, and interviews with men and women struggling with commitment issues. On a more personal note, we feel uniquely qualified to address this problem not only as therapists, but also as women, wives, and mothers.

"Men *want* relationships," one male client told us, "but they don't want to work at them." This is true for some men, but many are ready to take responsibility—and, as you'll see from the case histories we tell you about, many have not only reacted enthusiastically to our ideas but also volunteered their own stories for this book. "I feel empty inside," one man said thoughtfully. "I'm lonely." And he is typical of the men who know something is missing from their lives and who are starting to look into their own hearts for answers.

No man is born unto himself alone,
Who lives unto himself, he lives to none.
—FRANCIS QUARLES, *Esther*

Part One

COLD
FEET

1

Identify Your Guy

There's a new guy in town. You've met him. He's everywhere. He's the computer analyst next door, the lawyer who gives you business advice, the guy behind the deli counter, and your best friend's husband. He's the guy you work with, go out with, live with . . . he's the New, Uncommitted Man. What is new about him? On the surface, quite a bit. He's sensitive. He tries to understand you. He wants a woman who is his equal. He wants intense lovemaking and intellectual challenge.

At first, he seems to be the kind of guy who'd be easy to love. But it doesn't quite work out that way. Women who get involved with the new man soon find out that appearances are deceiving. His warm heart and warm body can't change the fact that this guy has cold feet.

How does it feel to be him? Since most men feel safe enough to open up in therapy sessions and interviews, we can give you a good idea. When you come right down to it, a man is likely to start sweating as soon as you say *intimacy*. The problem has to do with personal boundaries. As people in relationships get closer, the boundaries of the self become more diffuse, more permeable—for men, this natural process is a problem. Now we're going to ask *you* to do something difficult. Tell yourself that the problem you've had with men isn't *your* problem! Women—all of us—are so used to blaming ourselves and protecting men that we have to wrench our minds around to see it any other way. But you can learn to see it differently. That's why we want you, while reading this book, to go against some of your deepest instincts. We want you to begin to look at men—and at yourself—in an entirely new way.

See Him With Your Head—Not Your Heart

When a man has cold feet, the first thing a woman should do is step back and take a cool view of the situation. Often, women "think with their hearts": "Love will make it right," we say, or, "I was swept away!" Once you realize that men are raised to assume that women *live* to meet their needs and that male fantasies about women often involve an endless sexual smorgasbord, you'll also see how dangerous it is to romanticize relationships or leave them to your instincts. These days, love means using your head, as well as your heart. Even if—*particularly* if—you've been swept away, you still have to look at a man objectively. If you don't, you will see only what you want to see—not what is really there.

What To Look For

Spotting men with cold feet can be easy—once you know what you're looking for. Does he:

> 1. think you're "too demanding"? even, "too sexually demanding"?

2. think you "pry" into his life?
3. blame you for everything that goes wrong?
4. tell you that you invade his "space"?
5. resist planning ahead for dates?
6. resist thinking of the two of you as a couple?
7. resist "accounting" to you for his time?
8. like to keep his "options" open?
9. think of the relationship as a ball and chain?
10. get angry or turned off when you talk about your problems or concerns?
11. always have to keep things light on dates and accuse you of "getting heavy" when you bring up anything serious?
12. have temper tantrums when he doesn't get his way?
13. expect you to pamper him?
14. feel threatened by your work success?
15. seem to need instant gratification (any woman who strikes his fancy is fair game)?
16. believe that somewhere there is a "perfect woman" waiting for him, and that he is entitled to have her?

Think about an individual man's behavior—do any of these points sound familiar? To help you read him we've outlined in detail the three kinds of men who fear commitments, beginning with the Good Enough Guy (and even *he* has certain problems), then moving to the man in the middle, the Good Guy Today/ Gone Tomorrow, and finally ending up with the Good For Nothing Guy, the most lethal man on the spectrum: the one whom you can just forget about. A large number of men toward the good-enough end of the spectrum *can* learn to make emotional commitments to women. We will help you evaluate those who can and those who can't, won't, and never will.

Remember: a man who seems to be a sure thing may turn out to be the world's worst bet. A man who appears to be a hopeless case may actually be able to learn and grow. After you've read further and have begun to apply new skills, try the same test.

The Good Enough Guy

"I don't want a Good Enough Guy!" said one woman during a women's workshop on men's intimacy problems. "I want a *great* guy!"

All of the women in the workshop were up in arms. It was practically a mutiny. No one wanted a guy who was only . . . good enough. What a letdown.

And from one Good Enough Guy: "What do you mean I'm not a great guy?" He said that he felt demeaned by the term—he was doing the best he could to be responsible and committed, and we were telling him he *still* didn't measure up! "You're judging men against a female standard," he argued. "Do you want men to be like women?"

Women *are* experts in intimacy; as little girls we learned our skills at our mother's knees and through our socialization. Later, we honed these skills in our relationships. Unfortunately, at this time, men can't be more than "good enough" at intimacy for the chillingly simple reason that no one ever taught them how to be better! So a man can be a first-rate mountain climber, cook, or college professor, but when it comes to intimacy and emotional commitments, he won't be up to par with you.

You've probably read a lot about how men can't "open up" and express their feelings. But we're not talking about self-expression—we're saying that most men lack the *radar* for emotional connection that women have. "Opening up" is only step one—a man may pour out his heart and end by saying he needs more space. This isn't good enough! He needs to learn how to have his space *and* be intimate at the same time. Fortunately, many men are now learning from women, but women shouldn't expect miracles. Keep wanting and aiming for the best—keep wanting a great guy—but realize that even those men we call Good Enough have a long way to go in this regard.

We told the group that all men fear intimacy, but that this fear comes in three different-strength doses. The Good Enough

Guy has the mildest dose—he fears a loss of *freedom* in a relationship. Most men feel entitled to have everything they want, emotionally, from a woman—without giving up anything to get it. Giving something up (such as dating many women) to get something else (a monogamous relationship) may make him chafe at the bit. Most women know they have to make trade-offs; to men—even Good Enough men—this is an outrage!

William has a romance about his past, a time when it seemed to him that "sex was just a phone call away." Then, at one point in college, Wiliam had what he calls a personal awakening—or else just a bad depression. He'd accomplished everything he'd set out to—he was popular with women, a good student, and a fine tennis player. What was left? For six months, William withdrew into a shell. His only friend was a brilliant gay man from one of his classes; the two spent hours talking about their families, their feelings, and their problems.

William began to spend more time studying and less time playing—and decided to move to New York to begin a career. But when he first landed in the big city, he got a job at a large department store. "I was a young buck," he says, laughing. "I had my pick of all the women who worked there!" But now, after his period of soul searching in college, William's relationships were "less fleeting, more human." For the first time he went out with a woman steadily for a year—a bright, attractive woman who ended up becoming attached to him. "She needed more support than I was able to give her," William says. "I had a tendency to eat women up. I wasn't happy about it, but I broke up with her. To me, this relationship was a trial run; I wasn't willing to make a long-term investment."

For the next two years, William played around. "The relationships I had were based entirely on sex," he says, "but I denied it to myself. I didn't feel as if the women had expectations, but maybe I never let myself investigate it because it was uncomfortable for me."

Then he met Marie. "She was funny, attractive, and smart," he says. "She wasn't the most beautiful woman I'd ever dated, but she had an energy. . . ." William knew he really liked Marie, but he also knew this made him nervous. "I'm seeing a lot of women," he told her, and warned her not to break up with anyone on his account. Meanwhile, the two did not go to bed—unheard of for William. "If you think of someone totally sexually at the beginning," he says, "it changes the potential." Somewhere in him William knew there was potential—and he didn't want to blow it.

A few months later, Marie broke up with the man she was seeing and began to get more involved with William. William, meanwhile, continued to see other women—until the day Marie said, straight out, "It's me or them."

Stunned, William hemmed and hawed. Then he said, "I'll have to get back to you on that!"

Being with Marie meant a major trade-off. Most men have a gut response to the very idea of monogamy: *ouch.* It means, at least initially, giving up *way too much.* For women, monogamy doesn't hurt—generally, we want to stop shopping around and revel in a good find. (Oddly, men aren't loathe to make trade-offs in business—there, it's called using your best judgment, going for it. Unfortunately, it's *emotional* trade-offs that are hard for men to swallow.)

But William searched his soul. No woman had ever said this to him before, and Marie's words had suddenly made everything clear. His "other women" were not worth the sacrifice of Marie.

Was it worth it? Absolutely, William told us. And how did it work out? "Not a day goes by when I'm not attracted to another woman—at the office, at a party, on the street—but I just don't act on it," he says. "Giving up the other women was like giving up a smoking habit: hard, but the best thing I ever did."

Then Marie upped the ante again. They were spending too much money on cabs and the hours they kept were crazy. Why didn't they start living together? Again, William was thrown. He'd only recently managed to get his own apartment, which was, he says, "like an icon" for him—a symbol of his independence and professional success. And just the thought of having his own space was so important—it made him break into a sweat to imagine being with Marie all the time, without an escape hatch.

The important difference between William and many other men is that twice, in spite of his cold feet, he made trade-offs. A male prerogative (especially of a young, handsome man like William) is to binge on the sexual smorgasbord until he's stuffed. Another part of a man's prerogative is to have a space of his own. But with Marie, William didn't feel trapped. Even though the timing wasn't quite right for him, his relationship with Marie came first.

We told William that his natural way of moving into an intimate relationship set him apart from almost all the other men we'd interviewed. But Marie's role was critical. "She knew what she wanted and she said it," William told us. "I had so much respect for her—her decision to say these things took more guts than either of my decisions. She helped me decide. After that, she became even more attractive to me."

Marie, like most women we see, wants more from relationships than ever before. And why shouldn't she? She has a lot to offer and a lot to lose if she settles for less.

It's upsetting to most women (including us) to realize that they will not meet a man for whom intimacy is second nature. When we thought about the disappointment women expressed at the very idea of the Good Enough Guy, we recalled the concept of the Good Enough Mother, developed during the 1950s by English psychoanalyst Donald Winnicott. He introduced a new way of describing the mother's role: a child can have a basically caring, nurturing mother who isn't perfect. A child doesn't need an ideal mother in order to grow up happy and healthy, Winnicott maintained: all she or he really needs is a mother who is good enough.

Men are neither perfect nor perfect monsters—there is a middle ground. Good Enough Guys can make commitments—even if they have problems *living in* relationships. They don't like giving up their freedom, they may try to get everything their own way, and they may ask for a lot of attention from you without returning the favor. The Good Enough Guy is no Boy Scout.

But at the bottom line, the Good Enough Guy respects you;

he's self-reflective and secure enough to admit that he has problems. He isn't allergic to apologizing, making trade-offs, and taking responsibility.

Lenny told this story about himself. He and Michelle had planned to have dinner together at home, and, after work, Lenny stopped to pick up some take-out Chinese from a neighborhood restaurant. All day, he'd been looking forward to this evening alone with Michelle (often they both worked too late to eat together), and once at home he eagerly set the table and started to light the candles. Just then the phone rang. Already irritated, Lenny picked it up. It was an urgent business call for Michelle.

Lenny wanted to tell the caller to call back tomorrow—this was his time with Michelle, and he was more important than business—but he knew this wasn't really fair, so he went to the bedroom to tell her about the call. Half expecting her to say she wouldn't take it, he was furious when she went immediately to the phone. For a few minutes, he hovered around her—"Make it fast," he mouthed—then, after ten minutes, he signaled her in exasperation. Distractedly, she waved him away.

Angrier than ever, Lenny wandered into the kitchen. He'd figure out some way to make her feel guilty, he decided; he'd tell her not to bring business home to dinner. But suddenly, Lenny realized that he was pouting and scuffing his feet like a two year old, and that when business calls came for him at home, he always took them, no matter what else was going on. He was accustomed to having Michelle accommodate herself to him. Shame-faced, he got out the food and put out two plates and the best wine glasses. By the time everything was ready, Michelle was off the phone, and as she walked into the dining room Lenny lit the candles. "So," he said, "everything okay with the Evans account?"

And he listened to her description with real interest.

Lenny is a Good Enough Guy, even though it is not always easy for him to accept the fact that Michelle has her own life (and that he's not always her first priority). Basically, he does expect things to go *his* way and isn't crazy about making trade-offs. He enjoys being with an independent, professionally successful woman, but he has to give up the notion that this is a woman who will live for him. Lenny, like all men, was raised to believe that women would accommodate him. He may *try* to get away with the old stuff, but it's hard because Michelle won't let him. And he knows that if she did, he wouldn't really be happy with her anyway. Before Michelle, he was with a woman who usually let him have his own way. Compared with her, Michelle is "a handful. She can be difficult, and there's no b.s. about her. I like that better than a woman who just rolls over when you snap your fingers."

What makes a Good Enough Guy less fearful than other men? In a sampling of men in this category, we found that Good Enough Guys and their mothers tend to have a healthy respect for one another. As a child, this boy felt nurtured and protected by his mother, while also knowing how to protect himself *from* her. He had a well-developed sense of privacy—his own boundaries were firm. Usually, his father was remote, but the Good Enough Boy didn't take Dad as a model for male behavior; in fact, if he intuited that his mother was lonely and unfulfilled, he felt sympathetic to her. As an adult, then, this man is sympathetic to women and unthreatened by them—he will not perceive a woman as an engulfer or a space invader.

To return to our Good Enough Guy's question: "Aren't you judging men by a female standard?" In some respects, yes. There are no neuter, or neutral standards, and until recently women and men alike have been judged by male standards. Now we're saying that many men can learn from women how to take the sting out of intimacy, and that, in fact, "freedom" can be traded off for something far better.

The Good Guy Today/Gone Tomorrow

Warm hearts and (very) cold feet distinguish this category of men from the first. The man in the middle's most striking feature is that he *can* have a relationship—the big issue is that he may not be able to make a commitment. He is powerfully drawn to the idea of intimacy with a woman, but fearful of his own urges. He has a double dose of fear; more than a loss of freedom, he fears a loss of *identity*—when he gets close to a woman he feels as if he's losing pieces of himself.

Intimacy gives him the shakes. When he has to give up some of his activities in exchange for the relationship, he feels robbed. As far as he's concerned, you're a space invader, moving in and taking his territory. That's why you may find a man like this taking sudden, dizzying giant steps to stand apart from you. Let's say, for example, that the two of you have been getting closer— suddenly, you don't hear from him for two weeks. "I need more space," he says.

This man's "space" means a great deal more than his apartment. It is his psychic space that becomes overcrowded when he is in a relationship, and he constantly needs to lock a woman out in order to reassert his identity as a man and a person. He can get close but can't sustain the closeness.

The Good Guy Today/Gone Tomorrow is a new breed. In the past, social conventions of marriage and family concealed the conflicts many men had. Society frowned on relationships that didn't end in marriage, and when a man did marry he would be considered a "devoted" husband and father as long as he *looked* the part. These roles didn't require a man to be intimate—he simply had to go through the motions. Now that the old conventions have been exploded and men are no longer compelled to marry simply to fulfill societal and family expectations, the conflicted man no longer has any *motivation* to marry! In fact it is far easier for him not to. In the past, people dated with the idea of marriage in mind; now, for many men, dating is an end in itself. A man can date for fifteen years or longer and have four or five or more "meaningful" relationships, which he can break off as soon as a woman starts discussing a commitment. Many women say, "He would be great, if I could only get him to commit." That's a big "if only." It is possible that he will, but waiting around patiently for him to do so is futile. Other steps need to be taken.

Often, behavior in bed exposes this guy: at the beginning, while it's still "safe," he gives a lot; later, when you start to get close, he backs off—or even becomes sadistic. Many men complain about having to please women, in and out of bed, and many secretly wish women would just do it *their* way. But with the sexual revolution, women learned to be more aware of and more straightforward about their sexuality; in this category of men we are now seeing a backlash against women's new self-confidence.

Matthew, who is in his thirties, has been involved with Julie for several years. When they first met, he was up-front about himself; he'd had a number of serious relationships before her, but none had worked out. To be perfectly honest, he didn't know exactly what kind of woman he wanted. But he liked Julie quite a lot, and they clicked sexually, without a hitch.

But now they are locked into a vicious sexual cycle. "We fuck; we don't make love," Julie says bitterly. "It's all for him." She feels used and repelled; she's broken up with Matthew a number of times but has taken him back each time after a few months. At first, the sex is great, just the way it was at the beginning—but this never lasts, and the whole cycle starts over again.

Matthew can't say what the problem is, but he feels sure it has something to do with Julie. She is "too demanding," for one thing, and for another, he is sometimes attracted to other women. If she were really right for him, he wouldn't be.

At first, Julie believed Matthew. "It's embarrassing," she told us, "but I really am too demanding." We asked her to tell us just how demanding she'd been. "Do you want him to give up his life?" we asked her. "Are you asking him to kowtow to you?" Julie smiled and shook her head no.

"All you're telling Matthew," we continued, "is that you want good sex with him! Would you think *he* was too demanding if he asked that from *you?*" Julie saw that obviously she wasn't asking for anything so outrageous. (What we see in our practices is men telling women they are too demanding as a strategic move—to put it bluntly, it's a way of getting a woman to back down. A man's need to do this reflects his deep, primordial fear of "giving in" to a woman.)

Julie figured out that Matthew never thinks she's too demanding until he starts feeling close to her. So she told him that she thinks he's afraid to sustain the closeness they achieve through good sex. Not surprisingly, Matthew was somewhat put off by this analysis, but when he looked at the pattern of their relationship, he had to admit to Julie that he shuttled back and forth between closeness and distance.

At this point Matthew *could* make a breakthrough (at least he's willing to talk and admit his own difficulties)—or he could prove unable to face his problems. Breaking through means that Matthew must resolve his fear of the loss of his individuality or separateness. To make a commitment to a woman, a man must know who he is and that he won't be buried by her.

For her part, Julie, or any other woman in this situation, needs to know that she cannot break through for him. What she *can* do is to be clear and specific about what she wants in a relationship so that he doesn't think she is making across-the-board demands. For example, rather than saying that he must become a better lover or else, Julie might tell Matthew that she'd like him to spend more time kissing her neck and shoulders and caressing her breasts; she should explain that it takes her longer than it takes him to get aroused. He may still feel as if she's asking too much; if so, Julie has to figure out if this reverberates in other areas of their relationship. Sometimes a man's fear of "giving in" to a woman is only most obvious in bed.

We aren't fortune-tellers, and we don't know how this relationship will work out. In cases such as this, a woman has to hang out and *not know*—at least for a while. If Matthew continues to say she's too demanding, it's a good clue he won't make it. The first time it happens—or even the second—isn't necessarily the kiss of death. The point is that he should be getting better as time goes on.

It's easy to make mistakes about men in this category. When Debbie told Larry she was in love with him, his reaction was, "I like you a lot, but I'm not ready to commit." When her birthday came along, she told him that she wanted them to spend the whole weekend together, which was fine with Larry, except that one night there was a party he wanted them to go to together. Debbie refused—she wanted the whole weekend as *she* wanted it. Suddenly, they had a power struggle on their hands.

In a consultation with us she said she'd told Larry that either he spend the whole weekend with her or go to the party alone. "He's backing off from committing himself," she told us.

We said, "Wait a minute. Why do you think he's backing off? He's including you. And remember, you switched the rules on him when you said you loved him. He hasn't caught up with you! It seems as if you're forcing him to show he cares about you by giving up something he really wants to do. He's going to feel manipulated."

"But why should I do things *his* way?" she asked.

"Why is it *his* way when he wants to spend one night doing what he wants and one night doing what you want?"

"I don't think he's a guy who can make a commitment," Debbie said firmly.

"We don't think you have any evidence of that whatsoever," we told her, just as firmly.

We were at a deadlock. But after Debbie sat with these ideas for a few minutes, she slowly began to talk about the man who had dumped her two weeks before their wedding. With him, she'd made no demands at all. She'd done everything his way. Now maybe she was compensating for that—a little too hard. Maybe, too, she was trying to destroy her relationship with Larry before he had a chance to leave her, as her fiancé had.

A week later, we got a phone call from Debbie. She felt great, she said. After she'd met with us, she'd gone directly from our office to a pay phone on the street and called Larry. "I told him I'd been a jerk," she said. "I told him to forget everything I'd been saying about my birthday weekend. And he was completely understanding." We were delighted! But what had we said that sent Debbie flying to that corner pay phone at eight o'clock at night to call and make up with "the guy who couldn't commit"?

We'd asked her, she said, how she would feel if Larry had agreed to do it all her way. All the way downstairs in the elevator, she had mulled this over. "I knew it would have felt lousy," she told us, "a real Pyrrhic victory. I was jeopardizing the relationship for no reason."

If you've been badly burned in a previous relationship, it's important to realize that you are probably defensive and mistrustful, and possibly prone to acting too fast. Two simple rules are: With the Good For Nothing Guy (whom we'll talk about next), know who he is and get out fast. For the Good Guy Today/Gone Tomorrow, we say you have to be careful. Give it time. Observe him over the next two to three months. Does he blow hot and cold? When and why? Don't jump into bed too fast—and don't push him *out* too fast, either.

If a relationship is to succeed, a couple has to mesh, like a complex, beautifully constructed machine of many parts. Timing is crucial to the functioning of the machine: if the timing is off, then no matter how well suited the parts may be, there will be a clashing of gears.

Joan and Keith were out of synch, and as a couple they broke down. From the beginning Keith was straightforward with Joan. He liked her, but he simply wasn't ready to make a commitment. Meanwhile, Joan so much wanted him to commit to her that she pressured him, hoping for a change of heart. Keith didn't want to lie or misrepresent himself, so he told her that he *might* be ready in five or six years, but now was just too soon for him. For Joan, who was 34 (Keith is 29), this was out of the question, and she broke up with him.

Keith's capacity for commitment is almost impossible to gauge; at age 29, his "too soon" may be just an excuse. At age 34 or 35, it will definitely be an excuse. At any rate, when the timing is off, a man's capacity for intimacy is off—if you're on different timetables, don't linger. A guy who is really good enough will make a commitment even if the timing isn't ideal for him.

Joan is typical of many women in their thirties who want marriage and children but are involved with men who "aren't ready." We've heard plenty of criticism of women who delay starting families—it isn't smart, women are told, to leave it all until you're in your thirties. Forget the criticism. All the research on the subject shows that the older you are when you get married, the likelier you are to stay married. If you'd married earlier, statistically you'd probably be divorced by now and be the sole support of two or three kids. If all this sounds like a disaster story to you, you're right. It's smarter to get your career in order and figure out what you really want in a man before making rash decisions you might live to regret.

Even though you can't change a man's timetable any more than you can change your own, you can learn important ways to synchronize when both of you are willing. In the next chapter, when we discuss the Five Levels of Commitment, we'll talk about timing, trade-offs and temporary detours.

The Good For Nothing Guy

Not only can't this guy make a commitment, he can't even say the word *relationship* without choking! In a workshop session, one woman talked about a man who'd occasionally spend an intense, passionate weekend with her. Afterward, no matter how much they'd enjoyed each other, he wouldn't call her again for weeks. "If I could only get him to make a commitment," she said, "things would be so great!"

"But this has been going on for months," we pointed out. "Obviously, he *can't* make a commitment."

"But he's so affectionate when he's with me!" she insisted.

"So why doesn't he call you?" asked another woman in the group.

"I asked him the same thing," she replied. "He said he was sorry about that, and then he said—you're going to laugh—well, he said, 'boys will be boys.' "

At this, every woman in the room burst out laughing. "Right," we said, "boys will be boys, but you want a grown man!"

She was laughing, too—but mad as hell.

Listening to a guy like this and taking him at face value is like believing the packaging on the diet pills that promises "Lose twenty pounds in two weeks!" The Good For Nothing Guy is smooth, good-looking, charming, and disarming. If you want a relationship with this guy, forget it. If you're looking for commitment, forget you even *thought* about it.

When one woman jokingly talked about buying the latest

issue of a women's magazine and reading all about "How I Can Nail My Man," everyone laughed. We think it's good to laugh, because advice like this *is* a joke. The Good For Nothing Guy will *never* be nailed! There are only two things you can do with a guy like this: 1) walk away; or 2) have good sex with him (which also means *safe* sex) and *then* walk away.

The Good For Nothing Guy has an extra-strength dose of fear. We call it the fear of engulfment. For a man who is literally afraid of being swallowed or eaten alive (typical terms that such men use to describe how they feel), having a relationship is the equivalent of psychic death. He has no clear sense of where he stops and you begin. This man is knocked out by the strength of his fear—he will never be able to have a relationship with a woman. His behavior will always tell you, "No!"

Sometimes women want to kill us when we say a man is good for nothing. It is angering and disappointing to see a man for who he really is—and it is heartbreaking for us because we see that women want so much to believe these guys are better than we know they are. We've learned about these men through experience, and we've been just as shocked as other women at the number of men out there who can't make commitments—or relationships. Reading a Good For Nothing Guy's behavior is critical for a woman who wants to cut her losses and get away fast.

Roz didn't want to see the truth about Brian, so she ignored all the signals and went full steam ahead toward disaster. The week that she met him in an art gallery, she was bubbling over with excitement. On the day she'd met him, Brian, in his early forties, was dressed in offbeat clothes—orange T-shirt, black jeans, and orange socks—which gave him a pleasingly funky appearance. He'd been immediately charming and attentive and had made a date to see her the following night. On their first date, the two had dinner, then went back to Brian's apartment. Roz said that she'd been anxious and conflicted. She loved sex (and hadn't had any lovers for a while), but she also knew that she wanted a commitment from a man.

By the couch, she saw a note that listed her name and two other women's names. Yet, Roz didn't see how she could be just one of three women Brian was pursuing. He'd been so attentive to her all evening, telling her funny stories and complimenting her on the unusual necklace she was wearing. In her experience, most men would have been too self-centered to notice.

By now, Roz was swept away. Still, she wasn't sure if she was ready to go to bed with Brian. If this was to be a "real" relationship, it was too soon for sex. When she explained this to him, Brian was very understanding, but when she left, he didn't offer to walk her downstairs to get a taxi. This bothered Roz, but she dismissed it by telling herself the poor guy was tired.

After that night, Brian was in hot pursuit. On their next date, Roz still hadn't made up her mind about sleeping with him, but Brian was very tender with her, spending a lot of time kissing and caressing her. This won her over; of course he must care about her. That night, they had hot, exciting sex.

In the morning when Roz got up, Brian was already working at his desk. She showered and tried not to make too much noise as she got dressed. "Will you call me soon?" she asked nervously. "Sure," said Brian without bothering to look up. But her "soon" and his "soon" were in two different time zones. When four days went by and he didn't call, Roz panicked. Why didn't he call? What had she done wrong? Was he seeing one—or both—of those other women? When he finally did call, she was so relieved that she said nothing about how he'd made her feel and invited him to a party. Brian agreed to meet her there—then didn't show up.

Not only has Brian hidden his terror from himself and the world but he has successfully finessed it into culturally sanctioned male behavior—Brian is a good-time guy. He can literally charm the pants off a woman—he has a knack for knowing what to say and what to do. For him charm is the key to control—the means by which a frightened man gains power over women.

But even though she understood this, Roz felt taken. She'd misread all the signals, which should have been so obvious. "If a friend of mine had told me about Brian, I would have told her to dump him right away!" she told us. "He was *horrible*. How could I have been so stupid?"

She isn't stupid. None of us are stupid. You may be a whiz

at seeing your friends' mistakes, but when you are the one who is involved, it is never so obvious to your own heart. We worked with Roz to identify the clues she'd overlooked so that she would be able to identify possible (and probable) Brians in her future and get the information she needs—in time.

Unfortunately, Brian isn't the only kind of Good For Nothing Guy. Another type we've seen is so terrified of engulfment that he plays a cat-and-mouse game with a woman. He may, for example, call you and make a date, then break the date. This may happen a number of times. Or he may tell you after you've been going out for a while that he really needs to be alone, or that he's been seeing someone else. It shocks you, and you wonder what you did to drive him away, but it's his fear that's in the driver's seat. For example, one man was so phobic about commitment that he wouldn't even tell his girlfriend where his office was! Soon after, he left her so that he could be alone—he only feels *alive* when he's single.

A man like this may arouse your sympathies—it is very sad when a person is too frightened to love and be loved—but the fact is, you can't change him. Don't wait or wonder or try to "bring him out"; he is an emotional hermit and he's better off hiding beneath his rock.

A third variation on the theme of the Good For Nothing Guy is the outright sociopath (although you may hate to think of a man you know in this way). A good-time guy usually won't hurt you—unless you let him—whereas a sociopath will lie to you and use you for all you're worth. This man may be most easily identified by the fact that he sees other people strictly in terms of their usefulness to himself. He has turned his terror of engulfment into exploitiveness, and he has no conscience.

Mark would show up at Jill's apartment at three A.M. If she ever suggested to him that he come earlier—she often had meetings at work first thing in the morning—he'd suggest she was uptight. Usually, he'd be drunk or coked up; they'd have sex, and then he'd pour out his heart to her. He was so touching, so poignant, and made himself so vulnerable to her. Most men never talked about their feelings! So she'd stay up all night with

Mark, and she'd be bleary-eyed for days. But Mark always assured her that he loved her and needed to be with her, so it was worth it. Most of his possessions were in her apartment, and then he began to carry on his drug transactions there and to use her phone to make long-distance calls. Then she found out that Mark had been kicked out of his own apartment months ago. Apparently, he'd been using her place all along as a rent-free shelter—and fooling her by saying that he loved her. She put his stuff out on the curb and changed the locks on the doors.

Many women get hooked by Brians and Marks—and it is all too easy to blame these women. All of us have heard the same tired, old, *wrong* observations: "She has low self-esteem so she picks rotten guys . . ." "She has a lousy father so she picks lousy men . . ." "She's smart at work, but dumb about men . . ." The litany goes on and on. But we don't find it strange or self-destructive when a woman like Roz is attracted to a man like Brian. About five years ago we began to notice in our practices that as relationships became more intense and more egalitarian, men became more confused and confusing. So we can sympathize with women who find it hard to read all of this new behavior!

"Don't you think he'll change?" one woman asked about a Good For Nothing Guy. They were business acquaintances, and she didn't want to face facts when he'd have his secretary call her instead of calling her himself. She just wouldn't let it compute that he'd gone on to his next fling. "Gina," we said, "you've just got to see what this man is good for—he's rich, successful, good-looking, and fun. It should be a roll in the hay for you, catch as catch can, have a good time, go on the expense account—but *don't* break plans for him, *don't* make future plans with him, and *don't* go out of your way for him. Don't ever, ever, on any account or for any reason, take him seriously!"

"Don't tell me that!" is often a woman's first response—while at the same time she feels a tremendous relief. It's always painful to give up an old wish. For a woman, the end of innocence comes when she stops believing in the prince of her dreams and realizes that real men have all-too-real problems.

But women are making progress. For example, recently one

woman client figured out a Good For Nothing Guy in a mere three weeks. He would call her at eleven P.M., after he'd finished work and say, seductively, "I'd love to see you." (Translation: "I'm horny.") Twice in a week, she got into a cab and went to his apartment.

"But that's outrageous," we told her. "Why should he call you at eleven and expect you to jump out of your bathrobe and race across town in a taxi?"

She thought it over. "If he wants to see me," she decided, "he can damn well make a date with me at a respectable hour." Since this guy couldn't manage it, she stopped seeing him.

As fewer women put up with good for nothing behavior, fewer guys will get away with it. The next time a man like this comes into this woman's life, she'll say no the first time around. The point is that now that she *knows* the three categories of men, she can read their behavior more accurately. Someday she'll meet a Good Enough Guy who can commit. And she'll know the difference—we're sure of it.

Throughout this book you will need to remember that a man will only see his fear of commitment as a problem if *you* see it, name it, and insist on it. Otherwise he will be all too happy to blame you for the fact that the two of you just can't "get it together," and *he* will set the terms of your relationship.

A man who is finally able to make a commitment is a man who has identified the positive benefits of commitment for *himself*. This is a man who will find that he *can* be vulnerable, *can* take responsibility for himself and the relationship, *can* take on the challenge of a woman who is his equal. Not only can but *wants* to—because doing so makes him less fearful, less lonely, less conflicted. What we will do is help women identify the men who are unhappy enough to want to change, and then provide women—and men—with the techniques to bring that change about.

WHAT TO LOOK FOR

GOOD ENOUGH GUY	GOOD GUY TODAY/ GONE TOMORROW	GOOD FOR NOTHING GUY
Gets close and sustains it; you are in a relationship with someone who cares. May hesitate to make first move sexually, initially may even be impotent.	Sex starts out great but gets worse as the relationship progresses.	Can turn the charm on and off with the flick of a switch.
Expects a lot from you but doesn't automatically reciprocate (will sometimes take you for granted).	Blows hot and cold; you don't know where you stand.	Comes on very fast initially.
	Obsessed with protecting his independence and private time.	Great sex but no follow-through (you don't hear from him for a week).
Accepts trade-offs (will spend time with you instead of friends) but reacts to loss of freedom. Accepts some responsibility for problems the two of you are having.	You are always accommodating his schedule. Blames you for problems.	Says things like "boys will be boys" when you confront him with his lack of consideration.
	Fears "giving in" to a woman.	He'd be great "if only" he'd commit (the "if only" is a major stumbling block).
May be a slow starter—usually waits for signs from you that you are interested.	Withdraws after you've had a wonderful time together.	

WHAT TO DO

GOOD ENOUGH GUY	GOOD GUY TODAY/ GONE TOMORROW	GOOD FOR NOTHING GUY
Give him definite signs of encouragement. Love him and accept his limitation. Teach him about reciprocity in relationships (see chapter 7, "Relationship Strategies"). Make realistic demands for more involvement (for example, ask for more caressing during sex, or that he let you know ahead of time that you'll be spending the weekend together). Enjoy him—he's the best type of guy, and he *can* commit!	Discuss your sex life (emphasize your disappointment). Be vigilant—you can't afford to overlook signs of his ambivalence. Make realistic demands—see if he responds. Let him know that you like private time also. Listen to both sides of his ambivalence—not just the side you want to hear. Let him know you'd like to make plans ahead of time. See how he responds. Ask yourself: Is this relationship good enough for me? If your answer is no, break it off. If yes, read below. Shift the relationship to a lower level (see chapter 2, "The Five Levels of Commitment"). See if a more casual relationship works for you.	Dump him immediately *or* have great (safe) sex—*then* move on. (Do not linger with this guy—you'll wind up getting hurt.)

[24   ]

2

The Five Levels
of Commitment

Now that we've talked about the three types of men and why they
behave the way they do, we are going to introduce the Five
Levels of Commitment for you to use as a general frame of
reference for any relationship you are in. Then, for the rest of the
book, we will be applying the levels of commitment as a guide
to building modern relationships.

Why do we need a framework? Because things used to be
simpler—there were rules to follow. First of all, men and women
had clear-cut roles; they fit together like puzzle pieces and
unquestioningly filled in each other's lacks. Courtship followed a
prescribed linear progression: first you went out, then you held
hands, then you kissed goodnight, then you necked (above the
waist), then—maybe—you petted (below the waist), but you
didn't "go all the way" until you were safely married. You knew
how serious your relationship was by what you did and didn't do,
and marriage was assumed to be your goal.

But when sex no longer meant "commitment" (in the old

sense of the word), and couples started going to bed the first or second time they went out, many women were given a false sense of what a relationship really was. (Usually it was no more than a night in the sack.) Still, even in the age of AIDS, when people are much more cautious about whom they sleep with, we simply can't go back to the old ways of courting. Sexual behavior is as confusing as ever, and is in fact a wildly inaccurate indicator of the "seriousness" of a relationship.

Without an assumed "goal" at the end of a relationship, you practically have to be clairvoyant to evaluate its "seriousness." Even if marriage is your goal, you still have no guideposts to help you foresee if this is a relationship that will go the whole way, particularly since you probably spent your early twenties or all of your twenties having fun in various dating situations. Fun, you realize now, is only part of the story.

Now that the earmarks from the past are irrelevant, and anything-goes sexual freedom is outdated and actually dangerous, you need a wholly different standard to analyze the progress of the new, more complex relationship.

Working with couples is both an art and a science, and when we first began practicing, we didn't stop to articulate all of our assumptions. When we did, we told each other that yes, we assume that relationships progress in a sequence, and yes, we also assume that since relationships consist of two people, they might not be in the same place at the same time. From this observation we developed the Five Levels of Commitment, based on our clinical research and experience. Once we've described them, we'll tell you how to use them to assess the progress you're making in your relationship.

The Five Levels of Commitment

1. Dating

This is the level of zero commitment. At this point you are deciding if this guy is good for a good time only, or if he's good enough for something more serious. You are deciding what *you* want, and this is often the level at which most women feel they have the most control in the relationship.

When you are dating there is usually no regular pattern to the times when you see each other. If you like a man and are sexually attracted to him, you may quickly mistake lust for love. (After sleeping with him for the first time, you may find yourself lying awake, imagining introducing him to your friends, your parents . . . soon you're seeing yourself walking down the aisle next to him.) Men, on the other hand, rarely mistake sex for love, and unless a woman can enjoy sex without expecting a commitment from a man she's only dating, she should not have sex with him until she knows him much better.

We advise women who become emotionally involved early on to try to scale down their expectations, and not to jump into sex too soon. If a woman is already thinking about commitment, she may well tend to see only what she wants to see, and not what's really there. Having sex will not make a man—*any* man— any more or less likely to commit. A Good Enough Guy will wait—and he won't push you. Holding out won't necessarily make him want you more (that's an old ploy), but it won't turn him off, either. Will his ego be hurt? Maybe, but lasting, permanent damage is unlikely.

Always keep in mind: If you aren't the kind of woman who can engage in sex without strings attached, don't do it. Dating at this level doesn't *deserve* to be dignified by your calling it a "relationship." It isn't—*yet.*

2. Steady Dating

Let's say you've passed "Go"; the first level was good enough to make you feel ready for a relationship to unfold. Now you're counting on him a little more, expecting a little more; you see him with greater regularity. Basically, at this second level you're starting to become more comfortable with one another—getting to know one another beyond the formal structure of dating. "Do you want to come over tonight?" you might ask, and then the two of you will hang out around your apartment, eat take-out food, and watch TV. Or you might linger on a Saturday morning instead of getting on with your chores, or you might call each other during the day just to chat. The danger for a woman at this stage is that she will give in to the temptation to reveal too much of herself too soon. We call this the urge to confess—but if a woman thinks it will speed the pace of the relationship, she is dead wrong. If you find yourself yearning to bring out all the skeletons in your closet (you once had an abortion, you were fifty pounds heavier up until six months ago, you think you are falling in love with him), *don't*— there is a time and a place for such "confessions," but it is *not* at Level Two of commitment.

Many women assume that a relationship is moving toward monogamy (Level Three) before the word has even entered a man's vocabulary. A woman will tell herself, "Well, I'm not sleeping with anybody else, and I don't want to, so he probably feels the same way." Not so—monogamy is a giant step for men. Even though your guy may well *not* be seeing anyone else, if he has the *idea* that he's free to, he's still not monogamous—he's still on Level Two. Monogamy really is the *desire* to be involved with only one person.

At this point in Level Two, when you feel you're ready to progress to Level Three, you might bring it out into the open: "I'd like to invest something in this relationship. I want us both not to see anyone else." Listen very carefully to his reaction. If he doesn't say, "That's what I want, too," then you'll have to decide whether or not you will stay in the relationship. If he isn't ready to be monogamous, there is certainly no reason for you not to date other men. In fact, throughout these early levels of dating, there is absolutely no reason for you to see just one man. You don't know what the outcome will be, so why close out your options? Please keep in mind that we are not advocating promiscuity; you can certainly date as many men as you want without sleeping with *any* of them. And again, if either you or the guy you are involved with are seeing more than one partner sexually, *engage in nothing but safe sex.*

3. Monogamy

Monogamy can be a vague, amorphous, unspoken pact you've made; something you've "fallen into." In the first flush of passion and excitement at meeting someone you like, virtually anyone can be monogamous for at least a few months. Often, this doesn't last; you may find that he is being "monogamous" with several other women at the same time. True monogamy, however, is a big decision, and takes some talking about. This is when both people sit down and make a conscious decision to date and sleep with only each other.

True monogamy means far more than only having sex with one person. You are starting to build and develop a relationship. One sure way to distinguish true monogamy from the false is by noting how consistently he includes you in his life with his family and friends. If his friends don't know about you, and he doesn't even think of including you in activities he does with them, assume that your relationship is at Level Two. By now, you should have committed yourselves to the "we" pronoun, and other people in both of your lives should know that you have.

4. Monogamy Plus

You're a twosome, and you're accountable to one another. You plan vacations together or spend holidays with each other's families. Social invitations come addressed to both of you; friends wouldn't think of inviting one of you without the other to any kind of gathering, and both your families assume you're a couple. People ask you when you're getting married. Everyone seems to be waiting with bated breath for the date to be set.

At this level, you'll feel comfortable as a couple, even in potentially difficult situations. For example, if you are involved with a man who is divorced with children, by now he should include you in activities with his kids, and you should feel easy about it.

Monogamy Plus is often the biggest turning point for the guy with cold feet. Fortunately, many men who reach this stage survive quite well, even if they do show occasional twinges of discomfort.

5. Living Together

We go so far as to say, if you want to get married, living together first *could be the worst thing to do.* Couples may end up living together for all the wrong reasons at *any* level of commitment. Living together is too often misinterpreted as a necessary prelude to marriage. However, it is far from being a requirement for marriage, and it is often a major mistake to move in with a man without a commitment to get married. Of the three types of living together that we're about to describe, we're strongly opposed to two of them.

"He just graduated from law school and he doesn't have anywhere to live." "We're going together anyway, so why not?" In other words, living together for convenience. Living together is a serious matter, and you should not fall into it or just let it happen.

"Living together is an experiment . . . we'll give it a year and see if we break up or get married." Often people move in together with the thought that this will prepare them for marriage or let them know whether or not they'd work as a married couple. Our advice, basically, is to find out as much as you can without living together, since women are often the ones who come up short in this deal.

"We love each other, and we're committed to each other, but we don't believe in marriage." In some cases, living together still holds important symbolic value for at least one person in the relationship. Perhaps they've already had a disastrous previous marriage and don't ever want to risk repeating the experience. Or perhaps they are opposed to marriage as an institution. This can be a valid reason not to get married, and often couples in this situation will remain together just as long as if they were married, and indeed become common-law spouses with time. But this third situation is rare, in our experience, and before moving in with a man you should be very clear about the reason why you are going to live together.

Now that we've described the Five Levels of Commitment, we'd like to tell you how to assess which level you *think* you're at, and which level you're *actually* at, as well as how to deal with a man who stubbornly remains in, say, Level Two when you've been seeing the relationship in terms of Level Three or Four. Unfortunately, the couple cannot progress to further levels of commitment until *both* parties are ready and willing; therefore, it is of critical importance to be able to discern where your relationship actually is. Your relationship is by definition at the level of the less committed person—which is generally *his* level.

Keep in mind that skipping stages may be dangerous; it's better to build from one stage to the next. Often you will have to go back and *redo* a stage. The odds are that you are on one level while your partner hovers at another (and lesser) level of commitment. This is *not* disastrous—*if* you understand what's going on. Taking a backward step in a relationship doesn't necessarily harm it, nor does it mean that you're giving up. Sometimes *reverse* gets you to where you want to go.

Knowing the general levels of commitment can guide you through the mysterious, highly individual process of your own relationship; even though there are millions of cases, there aren't millions of stages—just different versions.

Now we're going to go over the stages more slowly and give you more information about what to look for and what to do.

You Are on Level One of Commitment—Dating—If:

1. You've gone out for several months, and you wish you could see him more frequently.
2. You've seen each other for the last six months, but your dates are always a matter of last-minute convenience.
3. You're excited because he's invited you to a big corporate shindig; unfortunately, he didn't invite you until the morning of the event. You suspect he really just needed an escort.
4. You're beginning to find that your Friday-night dates are lingering into Saturday afternoons. (This means you are *progressing* along Level One; you are *not* at Level Two at this stage!)
5. Sex is good—you can't complain—but you wish it were warmer and more personal.

[31]

6. You know you're going to see him over the weekend, but he won't tell you when.

7. He sends flowers to the office; then he's too busy to call you for two weeks.

8. When you call him for a casual get-together, it's often not convenient for him.

9. Yours is a long-distance relationship; you wait eagerly for his weekend visits, which are romantic and passionate, but nothing has changed for months.

10. Unfortunately, he can't manage to see you frequently during the week, but he does call you at home and at the office, just to chat. (Again, this is a sign that you are moving toward Level Two.)

Toward Level Two

Often a woman who has been dating a man for several months begins to assume that they're on Level Two—steady dating—when actually he's exhibiting many of the preceding behaviors which indicate that in *his* mind it is still just casually going out. You may be seeing one another with *some* regularity, say, once or twice a week—but not always on Saturdays. At this level you may not know what he's doing on the Saturdays he doesn't spend with you. At this point, you may be developing the embryo of a relationship, but it's still too early to tell. What can you realistically expect at this stage? Since a man will most likely be moving along the continuum more slowly than you are, you can't expect much. Does this conversation sound familiar?:

PETER *(Wednesday morning, as he departs):* "I had a great time. Let's get together sometime over the weekend."

JOAN: "Hmm, that sounds good. I'm free Saturday, if you are."

PETER *(balking):* "Well, I'm not sure yet about Saturday. I'll give you a call."

JOAN: "But I need to know when because—"

PETER: "What's the big deal? Let's play it by ear."

(Peter leaves.)

Joan and Peter had been seeing each other for five months at this point, and she'd *thought* they were almost on Level Three, monogamy. She certainly felt they'd been on Level Two for some time. But Peter's actions—putting her off when she tried to make plans a few days ahead, not introducing her to his friends, (even though she had introduced him to quite a few of hers) and refusing to come to her office when she wanted to show him where she worked—all indicated that he was still on Level One of commitment. Once she realized this, she decided to change her thinking about him:

PETER *(the following Thursday morning, leaving Joan's apart-ment):* "So, I guess I'll see you this weekend. I'll give you a call. Maybe we could see the new Woody Allen flick."

JOAN: "Well, actually, I already have plans for this weekend. Maybe some other time though."

PETER, *(taken aback):* "What do you mean you have plans! It's only Thursday!"

JOAN: "Peter, most people *do* plan their weekends a few days in advance. I don't like leaving it to chance."

Joan continued to make plans for herself so she wouldn't be sitting around waiting for him to call on weekends. It was hard at first because she *wanted* to see Peter. But finally he got the message and began calling her to make plans several days in advance. Of course Joan took the risk of having Peter never call her again—but if he wanted everything on only his terms, she reasoned, was he worth spending time with? Happily, Peter realized that Joan would not be available on his last-minute schedule. Since he wanted to see her regularly, he progressed to Level Two.

It is a temptation at Level One to want to find out who else, if anyone, your guy is seeing. However, this really isn't the right time to ask. This is also not the time to talk about "the relation-ship" to anyone except your *best* friends. At this point, many women tell all their friends and acquaintances they are dating someone, and this makes it even harder to deal with if things don't work out. One woman we know received a huge, gorgeous box of chocolates at the office from a man she'd been dating on and off; after sharing them with everyone in her office, she started frequently dropping his name. As it turned out, this guy disappeared soon after the candy did, and she was then in the position of explaining to one and all that it (whatever "it" had been) was all over.

The mere act of talking about a man makes him seem more vital to your life than he really is. Then, when he drops out before the next stage, you feel like a person who "fails" at relationships, particularly when people you don't even know all that well ask what you and your "friend" have planned for the weekend.

This is certainly not the time to bring up "the relationship" to him. Remember that it's not a relationship *yet,* and don't give him the opportunity to feel trapped this early on. Also, listen to him—does he talk about plans for the *not-*near future? Does he say he already knows what he'll get you for Christmas when it's only June? Does he make sure to reserve a weekend night with you early (because he knows otherwise you'll be "booked up" if he waits too late)? These are the signs of a Good Enough Guy who may soon be ready to move to Level Two.

Before going on to the next level, however, we want to emphasize that moving on to *any* higher level of commitment before a man is ready will probably backfire on you. What we're seeing among women clients is less patience for the *evolution* of a relationship. Women now have a sense that they can set their own pace and control their own lives; if they can effect changes in the workplace and in other areas, why not move a relationship from Level One to Level Three? A good reason why not is that the man is probably not ready.

A woman will tend to progress faster and more evenly through the levels of commitment, whereas a man may very well backtrack to a previous level. Because men are more frightened, they proceed more slowly, setting up one defense after another and trying not to confront the fact—sometimes until it is too late—that they have gotten in deeper than they wanted. A woman has to understand that these are gender differences; any man, even a Good Enough Guy, will exhibit a totally different style from hers as he moves through the levels of commitment.

Identifying which level the relationship is on will help you deal more clearly in your own mind with how to get him to progress.

Level Two, steady dating, is a very tricky area because it's so easy to blur the lines in your own mind between this level and monogamy, at Level Three. Yet there are many clear indicators that a relationship is only on Level Two:

1. After you've been having sex for several months, you've only had orgasms twice; when you tell him, he's unresponsive.
2. You go to his office to meet him for dinner; you hang around expectantly, waiting for him to introduce you to his co-workers. He doesn't.
3. He invites you to a special telecasting on closed-circuit TV at his favorite hangout to watch the hottest team in town; then he leaves you to your own devices while he hangs out with his buddies.
4. You like to stay at your place; he likes to stay at his. Now he's willing to stay at your place from time to time, but you really have to twist his arm.
5. Your father is sick and in the hospital, and you're depressed. He knows you're upset, but still goes to the hockey game that night.
6. Before he met you, he arranged with friends to rent a ski house for the winter. Now he says he wishes you could be included, but he still goes away many weekends, leaving you alone. Meanwhile, he doesn't want you to date anyone else for the duration of the winter.

Toward Level Three

It may be all too clear to a woman now that she is further along the continuum than a man is, and that she expects more. Unfortunately, she may have to make some hard decisions.

Amy had been seeing Gary for six months. Usually, they got together once on the weekend and once during the week. Amy enjoyed the fact that Gary was reliable; for instance, he didn't change his mind Friday about their date Saturday. However, if they ended up seeing each other Friday *and* Saturday, he got a little panicky. One day he told her, "This isn't a monogamous relationship. I'm not seeing anyone else now, but I *could.* I want that freedom."

We told Amy that even though she didn't like what she was hearing, Gary sounded like a straight-shooter to us, and that she shouldn't jump to any conclusions. Shortly afterward, he told her that he was really looking forward to marriage and children some day—but not until he was in his mid-thirties, at least. Amy's heart sank—what should she do? It's like a sales budget, we told her. Give it six months; if he tolerates more closeness, she can project into the future. If he doesn't, the prognosis is poor and perhaps she should cut her losses.

Our feeling was that Amy didn't have to like where the relationship was, but she did have to accept it. If she tried to pressure him into moving to Level Three, he'd be compelled to prove to himself and to her that he was free and autonomous—*not* monogamous. It was up to her to match his pace instead of expecting him to match hers. You can't *make* a man move faster. If the pace is too slow for you, and there seems no hope of change, you have to get out. But before you do, realize that you will have to spend longer than you'd like at each level. Do keep an eye out for signs indicating that he's moving in the right direction.

Also, remember that this is not the time to suggest a vacation together. At this level, a weekend in the country is more your speed. And if you do go away for a weekend and have a great time, you *still* aren't "a couple" at this point. You are two people who like each other and do things together that are fun—a Level Two in the scale of commitment.

Achieving Level Three is a very hard transition because it involves more than just sexual fidelity. Jumping from Level Two to monogamy is as big a leap in its own way as the leap from Level Four to Level Five, living together, and it can be just as big a mistake. In other words, a man's decision to have sex with only one woman and develop a deepening consistent relationship with her is tantamount to giving up a powerful addiction—he has to really know what he's doing, and *want* to do it. A man should think about this carefully; the decision to do it should be preceded by a period of contemplation. If he feels pressured, he may comply, but it won't last.

Are men the only ones who have trouble with monogamy? Of course not; women, too, need to be sure they are ready. Age has a lot to do with it: if you've had years of dating a number of men, you probably want one *person* in your life at this point, not dates. You have a good idea of what you do and don't like in a man, and you're interested in planning your future. Let's now say that you've been dating a man for several months, and you can see a future with him. You sense that this is a "real" relationship (there is a reciprocal system of expectations and responsibilities); before now, you've only been wishing it on yourself. You don't want to commit yourself to marriage at this point, but you do have in mind a long-term commitment. If he feels this way, too, then you are ready for a monogamous relationship.

If marriage is what you really want, it's difficult at this point not to skip ahead in your mind and think about it, but if you talk about the future with this man, we advise you to keep it general. You're still checking him out. Let's say you're out on a walk together, and you see a couple with a baby. He says, with a shudder, "I'd never want kids," or else he remarks, "I'd like to have children someday." Now you know something more about him—you should be listening for what he says to see if he views the future the same way you do. Does he want to live in the city or the suburbs? What are his ambitions in his work? If you do want to get married someday, although not necessarily to him, don't feel that you have to hide this fact. This is a time to learn as much as you can about each other.

At this level, it may suddenly hit a man right between the eyes that he is "getting in too deep." For the Good Guy Today/ Gone Tomorrow, sex may begin to deteriorate. He may flirt outrageously with another woman at a party or even have an affair.

Your previously affectionate and attentive lover may recoil if you reach for his hand at his best friend's thirtieth birthday party; he may say "Get it yourself" if you ask him to bring you a piece of birthday cake. He may, in fact, react with a snarl to anything that even hints at possessiveness.

But even if a Good Guy Today panics, you shouldn't. Treat all of this as lightly as possible; in fact, it's best simply to ignore this sort of behavior if it's pretty random and doesn't become consistent. Certainly, *don't blame yourself* for anything like this; realize that it's *his* problem. He is reassuring himself that he is still autonomous even though he is indeed "involved." Commitment is harder for him than it is for you; his behavior is serious only if it becomes a pattern. Don't let him hurt your feelings, and be as brusque as he is or else just ignore him when he occasionally lashes out. If this behavior continues, try to talk to him about it, but don't be surprised if he's unwilling to discuss it. He may not even realize that he's chafing under the closeness of the relationship, and he probably *won't* want to talk seriously because he's afraid of the emotions he'll reveal. The following checklist may show you signs that you're stuck on Level Three, and not yet ready to progress:

1. You haven't had sex for a while; this is disappointing, and you've been talking about it, but no progress so far.
2. When you sneak away together for a weekend, it's perfect, but when you get back, you fight.
3. Whenever you bring up a problem between the two of you, he tells you that you're overreacting.
4. Suddenly, sex deteriorates; he just isn't interested, or he's interested—but only in his own pleasure.
5. When you talk about issues between you, he hears you out but tries to convince you it's your problem.
6. His lease is running out in six months and he goes out looking for a new apartment, suggesting you come along to advise him about what *he*—not the two of you—will need.
7. You realize your relationship is only so-so, but being with him is better than being alone.

Level Four, Monogamy Plus, *can* be an easier transition; you just naturally include one another in your lives. At this point, however, a Good Guy Today/Gone Tomorrow may draw the line. If you've been monogamous for six months, and his company throws a party, this is the time to find out if he wants to include you. If he doesn't, you aren't at Level Four, even if you've been monogamous *for years.*

A man can shock you by suddenly not including you in things that you've been doing together for months. He won't want to bring you with him to his college reunion, for example; he wants to keep this area of his life separate from you. Or maybe he doesn't invite you to his family's Christmas dinner, even though you've been to family events before now. Or he may suddenly start finding fault with you, picking on qualities he formerly adored. There are very subtle differences between Levels Three and Four. If you see your relationship in the list below, you are not yet solidly in Monogamy Plus; you are still struggling at an earlier level.

> 1. You're planning a trip to Italy, and all of a sudden your phone calls are strained. He feels business pressures are building up and considers delaying the trip until he has to go to Italy on business by himself.
> 2. He used to love the way you kept things going at parties; now he criticizes you for being a loudmouth.
> 3. Suddenly he complains about your mother's calls when he used to enjoy talking to her for a few minutes before you got on the line.
> 4. You overhear him saying to a friend on the phone, "Of course I can meet you Friday. God, it's not like we're *engaged* or anything."
> 5. When you're talking to his housemate and you refer to next summer's vacation at their cottage, he gets a vague look in his eyes and changes the subject.

Moving from Level Three, monogamy, to Level Four, Monogamy Plus, is so much easier for a woman than for a man because

Level Four really signifies a serious commitment. Often couples skip Level Five, living together, and go from Monogamy Plus right into marriage. So be aware that no matter *how long* you've been monogamous, it doesn't necessarily mean that you're going to move on to being committed to one another on Level Four. It all depends on what level the man is on, and you must use this criteria to determine where he is before you can truly progress to Level Five or to a serious commitment.

Sandra had been seeing Terence for five years. An attractive, petite blonde, she was a successful account executive at an advertising firm in St. Louis. Terence was a freelance copywriter; they'd met through a job Sandra assigned to him. It seemed quite obvious to Sandra's friends that Terence was never going to be able to commit, and they tried to warn her in veiled terms over the years not to get her hopes up too high. He did move with Sandra to Level Three, monogamy (at least sexually), but never let her know ahead of time if they'd be getting together, didn't include her in his family's activities, and often was brusque and even rude to her in front of friends. Yet Sandra hung on; she truly loved Terence, and she believed that love could make anyone change.

Finally, when the date of their fifth anniversary arrived and he was "too busy" to get together to celebrate it, Sandra realized she was with a man who would never be able to commit to her, or even to treat her very well. She decided that they would have to go back to Level One, "just dating," and that she would start to seek out meeting other people and would let her friends know she was ready to be fixed up with new men. It was frightening to be out in the singles world again, particularly given all of the sexual scares and diseases, but she knew she had to do it. She began not counting on Terence, and he picked up the subtle difference in her behavior; she never asked him when they'd see each other and indeed often had plans for the weekend when he called.

Sandra went on several blind dates, ranging from disastrous to merely dull. Then one night she went to a party and one of her good friends introduced her to a man she said she'd had "in mind" for Sandra for some time—Rodney. Sandra liked him immediately but didn't want to get her hopes up; when he took her number before she left the party she told herself he probably wouldn't call. But he did, and they planned to have dinner that weekend. When Rodney picked her up for dinner he had in his hand a single rose. Sandra was so flabbergasted she simply stared. In all the years that she'd dated Terence she'd given so many hints that she'd love to receive flowers, and he'd never so much as picked her one in the park. And now this guy was handing her roses on the first date! It turned out to be a good omen. Rodney and Sandra hit it off; he was attentive and thoughtful, and eventually, a good and sensitive lover. (Later Sandra apologized for staring at the rose and told Rodney why she was so surprised. Rodney couldn't believe a man who'd been seeing someone for five years would never send flowers!)

But what is most interesting about Sandra's case is Terence's behavior once she became unavailable to him. In the beginning when she was first seeing Rodney she still went out with Terence occasionally; it was hard to cut this man out of her life, and she actually felt sorry for him as well. But the more she edged out of Terence's life, the more aggressively he pursued her. The previous Christmas, when she'd tried to get him off the couch to help her decorate the Christmas tree in her apartment, he'd remained silently watching television. That November he called to see if she wanted to go to a sing-along of carols, *four weeks away;* she told him she couldn't because she'd probably have plans with the new person she was seeing. He began calling her several times a day at the office; finally, she had to tell her secretary not to put him through. The final straw came on her birthday. She received a huge bouquet of flowers and, assuming it was from Rodney, opened the envelope. It was from Terence! Now, after he'd lost her, he was finally sending flowers.

All this was extremely confusing and frustrating to Sandra, but she realized that he was attentive *only* because she was unavailable. Now, she was a challenge! If she did go back to Terence he'd revert to his previous good-for-nothing behavior. It infuriated her that he would attempt to "lure" her to him in this manner, particularly since she *knew* he'd take her for granted again once she did return to him. But she was too smart for that, and also she was beginning to fall in love with Rodney. Terence hounded her for another month. Finally he called her one night and proposed. Sandra again felt sorry for him, but realized the extent of his almost pathological pursuit of her once he'd lost her. She told him she was going to marry Rodney and also told him not to call her again. Now, she is engaged to Rodney, and it looks as if their relationship will be a truly committed one, for keeps.

When you're involved with a man who treats you badly it can be even harder to get out of the relationship because your self-esteem sinks so low. It's difficult to see what is going on when you love someone, even if all your friends are hinting (or outright telling you) that the guy is a jerk. Keep in mind Sandra's story if you're stuck with a man who is barely even at Level Three and won't move on to Level Four.

Toward Level Five

Level Five, the final level of commitment before marriage, also needs special consideration. At one time living together signaled a couple's liberation; when you "shacked up," you flaunted all of society's most dearly held conventions. For a woman it was particularly freeing because she was showing herself and the world she could have sex without marriage; for the first time, women had a choice.

Now things are more complicated. Living together is not assumed to mean sexual liberation; now it often ends up meaning that a couple's expectations clash. You may, for instance, "fall into" living together when you're 26, but by the time you're 30, it's started to mean something more to you.

We've identified a trend we call the Wall Street Syndrome, in which a couple who both have high-powered jobs occupy the same apartment and the same bed but whose long hours and career absorption make them strangers in the night. One couple we've worked with for over a year live together in a small studio apartment and appear to have all the accoutrements of a "real" household: they share money, dishes, furniture, and the laundry. For all intents and purposes, they're a couple. There's only one problem: she decided she wanted more than a roommate, rocked the boat, and drove them into couples therapy. Now she is gradually coming to see that the present terms of the relationship are ideal for her cohabitant (he isn't even her lover; sex faded almost a year ago). At the same time she admits she is denying the reality; even when he refuses to allow her to meet his friends or business colleagues, she won't face the truth. Why? Because this woman is afraid of "possessive" men who will "take her over" and try to rob her of her independence; her nightmare vision of herself as a typical suburban wife keeps her from knowing that she is with a man who can allow virtually no degree of intimacy whatsoever. Should this couple be living together? Absolutely not. They probably shouldn't even be dating.

Sometimes people move in together to see whether or not they should get married. In an "experiment" such as this, the woman is usually the guinea pig. Margaret had dated Charles for only eight months before they decided to live together. Now they've been cohabiting for a year, and he still hasn't decided whether he wants to break up or get married. However, his *actions* are telling: with dinner guests present, for instance, he is apt to discuss his—not their—travel plans for the following winter, while Margaret sits there feeling like the hired help. Don't let a man make you wait with bated breath as he decides about your future. If you don't have a commitment from him before you move in, you certainly won't get it after he's seen your hairs in the bathroom sink. Those hairs—or something else, it hardly matters what—will give him all the excuse he needs to say no.

At the age of 34, and after several years at the Monogamy Plus level, Jessica gave George six months to make up his mind about marriage. But it was more than her age that propelled her toward an ultimatum: Jessica had become intensely involved with George's young daughter from a former marriage. "I'm involved with you and Emily," she told him. "It's time to settle things between us." When she moved in with George and Emily, she had a wedding date set for the following fall.

In fact, we recommend that you move in with a man *only* if you both plan to be married within a year—if you are 28 or older. Otherwise you may be giving up too much valuable time for meeting other people, only to find three, four, five, or more years down the line that the Good-Enough Guy you moved in with has turned into a Good Guy Today/Gone Tomorrow—and refuses to marry you, ever.

If one partner has already been through a horrible marriage and divorce, the situation can take special patience and understanding. Larry had had a disastrous marriage a number of years ago, and now he shied away from the "symbols" of marriage. At the same time, he loved Ruth, with whom he'd been living for three years, and was truly committed to her. Ruth, meanwhile, was beginning to talk about concretizing their relationship; she was 36 and wanted to have children. But the whole notion of marriage stuck in Larry's throat. We did point out to him that they were actually more committed to one another than many of the married couples we saw. But for Larry, the dreaded "M-word" was a very big deal. He felt that marriage would stereotype him, and that their relationship was fine as it was. Marriage is not a necessity if a couple can make a deep commitment to each other without it. In Larry and Ruth's case, living together is not necessarily an obstacle to eventual marriage.

In general, though, before you move in or he moves in with you, you should have an understanding about marriage—that it's on the way (and only one short step away). It is not an "experiment" to see how it will work out, and if you decide to move in together simply for convenience, that's fine, but be clear that that is *all* it is.

The following checklist contains some situations. Before you move in with him, do any of these sound familiar?

1. Everyone you know is pressing you about marriage, but you've already made your plans and have agreed not to tell

anyone until you're ready. (This is a good reason to move to Level Five.)

2. When you go on vacations together, you fight about how much time to spend shopping or going to museums; you can never agree or give each other space.

3. If you do live together, one of you plans to keep a separate apartment.

4. If you move in together, he's said he won't let you bring your furniture because it doesn't match his decor.

5. You're in love, you're committed, but marriage seems too conventional to both of you. (Again, a good reason to move to Level Five.)

6. You keep close tabs on who owes what money to whom. You have a functioning monogamous relationship, but no real sharing.

7. If you live together, you'll both be going your own separate ways; you probably won't wait up for each other at night or eat many meals together.

8. You've lived together for six months, but he still hasn't gotten around to putting your name on the mailbox or telling his friends that you're living together now. (You can be physically living together but your guy can still not be committed to Level Five.)

By using the Five Levels of Commitment, you will be able to tell where you are in a relationship, and by going back to his level you can restructure the way you deal with him. These five levels are tools for you *to pin down exactly where your relationship is.*

In chapter 3, we'll look at ways in which a woman takes the blame for a relationship that doesn't progress, how this actually *hurts* your chances to move to a further level of commitment, and how to teach yourself to avoid the pitfalls of this harmful self-blaming attitude.

THE FIVE LEVELS OF COMMITMENT

LEVEL	DESCRIPTION	IDEAL DURATION*	DEGREE OF COMMITMENT	WHAT TO DO
1. Dating	No regular pattern to times you see each other. You should begin to decide what you want and how you feel about him.	1–4 months	None	It's better not to sleep together if you think you'll become emotionally involved. Don't try to find out *overtly* if he's seeing other people. Don't talk about this man too much to your friends at this point. Scale down your expectations.
2. Steady Dating	You're getting to know each other and to know you like each other. You are more comfortable with each other. You are seeing each other with more regularity (e.g. calling each other for a chat, spur of the moment dates).	2–4 months	You know you like each other, but there's no real commitment, yet. You may be dating others.	Avoid the "urge to confess" (that you think you're falling in love, that you just had an abortion, etc.). You're *not* at Level 3 yet so don't close out your options as far as dating other men. Don't suggest taking a vacation together.

3. Monogamy	You are building a real relationship at this point and you have made a decision to sleep only with each other. A good time to check out how his values and goals mesh—or don't—with yours as you both learn who the other really is.	6 months–1 year	This is the first level that signals the beginning of a commitment.	Notice how often he includes you in activities with family and friends. This is a big step for a man—don't panic if he has *minor* freak-outs (doesn't call once or twice when he's supposed to, occasionally shows up late, or goes a few weeks when he doesn't see you as often as usual).
4. Monogamy Plus	You are including each other in your lives on a regular basis. You are a twosome. You vacation together. You have met each other's family and friends. You both feel comfortable as a couple. People ask you when you're getting married.	6 months–2 years	This signifies a serious commitment—many couples go directly from Level 4 to marriage.	This is often the greatest turning point for men with cold feet—if he begins to distance himself, suddenly needs "space" for long periods of time, or if you notice a great change in the way he treats you, take it as a *warning.* (For help, see chapter 7, "Strategies for Relationships.")

LEVEL	DESCRIPTION	IDEAL DURATION*	DEGREE OF COMMITMENT	WHAT TO DO
5. Living Together	You live together as a couple. Other people view you as all but married.	6 months–1 year	Enormous range: from none (just convenience) to a fully committed relationship. If you *both* don't believe in marriage as an institution, this *can* be a fully committed level.	Many couples move in together but still don't get married—living together is *not* necessarily a prelude to marriage. Beware of Wall Street Syndrome—couples who cohabit but never see each other because of busy schedules. Don't move in together "as an experiment." If you want marriage, there should be a clear, agreed-upon time frame.

Ideal Duration refers to *the best possible length of time* in which you can be involved with a man at each particular level. These are *not* hard and fast time limits, but merely a span of time by which you can gauge your relationship. Also, realize that duration varies with age: If you and/or your boyfriend are under thirty, you can expect to spend a longer time at each level.

3

Kicking the "What Did I Do Wrong?" Habit

"Do I expect too much from men?" "Am I too demanding?" "Am I too pushy?" "Did I say the wrong thing?" . . . "What did I do wrong?"

We call this the "What Did I Do Wrong?" Syndrome (women clients volunteered other names—for example, "When in Doubt, Blame Yourself" or "I'm Sorry, It's All My Fault"), but whatever you call it, it's passed from mother to daughter, as if it's in our genes. *It isn't.* Self-blame is a learned attitude, and it can be unlearned—once you know what you're up against.

Nina, at 29, is a film producer who is accustomed to flying off to locations to make commercials; it's all in a day's work for her to hang from the open door of a helicopter to shoot a site. She makes a salary of nearly $100,000 a year, and she's just put a down payment on a co-op apartment.

Nina dates casually (and a lot)—mostly men she meets through work—but lately, she's begun to get serious. She wants a deeper connection with a man, and a family, a warm, loving *personal* place they create together. Unfortunately, she meets no one as serious as she is.

Until Jack. He is warm and funny, a television news writer, 33, who loves his work as much as Nina loves hers. He is tall and almost gangly, with a casual grace about him that made her sure he'd played basketball on his high school team. (When she asked him if he did play ball, he laughed and asked her how she'd guessed the story of his life. "You're really tuned in to me," he told her.) Both of them are strongly opinionated and they argue a lot, but neither can outshout the other.

Nina and Jack are an intellectual and sexual match for one another; not only is the attraction between them electric, but they are also comfortable just hanging out together, lingering over dinner or in bed on a Sunday morning.

After a few months of dating, Nina has thrown herself into a big project at work. On a working weekend at the office, she calls Jack and asks him if he'd bring over some sandwiches for lunch—they can have a picnic on the roof. But Jack says no, it would disrupt his plans for the day. As Nina eats a sandwich alone at her desk, she's glad she's independent enough not to need a man to take care of her. Then she wonders why Jack couldn't have put himself out just a little. In spite of her crazy schedule, she always takes care of their dinners together. Why does *she* always have time for dinner—and for him? He can talk to her for hours about problems he's having at the studio, but if she mentions her problems, his eyes glaze over. And although he says he respects her professional success, he never asks her about her work and always feels put out when she has to travel for business. Is she expecting too much from him?

When the pressure at work heats up even more, she asks Jack if he'd run some errands for her and make late dinners for them. Jack agrees—reluctantly—but after a day he poops out. When she blows up at him, he is shocked. Why in the world is she angry at him? "You're just too demanding," he tells her. And he pulls back—she wants *way too much.*

Meanwhile, Nina has scared herself. "I'm too demanding," she thinks. "It must be my fault." But there's a stab of anger in her stomach—*why* is she blaming herself? *He* is the one who's been letting *her* down!

Why does Nina blame herself? The real question is: Why do *both* Jack and Nina blame *Nina?* The answers lie buried in the past.

Flashback: 1954. Susan and Henry, Nina's parents, fall in love, get married, and buy a small house in the suburbs. When Susan becomes pregnant, the couple celebrates the fulfillment of their most cherished dream: to have a family.

Every day, breadwinner Henry boards the commuter train for his office job. And, when the baby is born, Susan finds she loves to be a mother. Together, she and Henry are creating a warm, comfortable nest for a family. Susan and Henry may be young—only in their mid-twenties—but they are responsible adults, who will, with other members of the community, build a solid, safe world for their children to inherit.

A few years later: sometimes, Susan hates the fact that she never uses her mind—will she ever? Although she can't admit it to herself, she is beginning to find her marriage—and her life— dull and routine. She becomes pregnant with their second child.

Henry enjoys providing for his little family. With Susan standing loyally behind him, he feels strong and manly, and he has gotten a big promotion at work. But sometimes Henry feels trapped and restless—especially now that a second child is on the way. Then he's stung by guilt. Of course, he says nothing to Susan. To her, he seems remote and withdrawn, and she misses the old days when they were so close.

"What can I do to make things better?" is the constant refrain in Susan's mind. Frantic to please Henry, she struggles to become the "perfect" wife, the "perfect" mother, the "perfect" home-maker. She is always patient and never angry; her own needs come last.

After Nina, their second child, is born, Henry buys the family a bigger house and a bigger car. He is the model husband—or so it seems. He mows the lawn in summer and shovels the side-walk in winter. He doesn't cheat on Susan. But by now, Henry has a secret life—he buys "girlie" magazines and fantasizes that he is a man about town with an endless string of gorgeous girls at his beck and call. In real life, he feels pressured all the time: money, houses, cars . . . it is his duty to provide, isn't it? His dream is that someday, somehow, he will bust loose from the ball and chain of marriage and become a "free man."

Years later, after Nina and her sibling have left the nest, Henry has an affair with a woman half his age. Susan finds out. At that point Henry files for a divorce, leaving her the house, the car, and a big settlement.

Susan, stunned, devastated, and lacking even minimal job skills, sits alone in her spotless kitchen. I don't understand, she repeats to herself endlessly. She must have done something wrong. How could Henry have left her? They'd had a marriage; they had children . . . how had she failed to please him?

What had *she* done wrong?

The "What Did I Do Wrong?" Syndrome stretches right back to the nice little house (and others just like it) on that quiet suburban street of more than thirty years ago. To understand how a woman like Susan could end up sitting alone and abandoned in her kitchen, blaming herself for the death of her marriage is to see why her daughter Nina blames herself today, even though she knows it's nonsense. To understand how a man like Henry felt like a workhorse and longed for "freedom" is to understand why Jack, today, feels that commitment to a woman means giving up way too much.

In the decade before Susan and Henry's marriage, during World War II, many women brought home paychecks from traditionally male factory jobs; however, as soon as the men streamed back from Europe and Japan, breadwinning women felt it their duty to go home again. During the 1950s, order and stability were seen as antidotes to the disruption and uncertainty of the war years. Avoiding postwar trauma meant traditional family values and clear-cut roles for women and men.

In the 1950s the home become "The Home," glorified and sacrosanct, a temple of safety, warmth, and love in a dark, frightening world. And women, with a small, subversive taste of independence still lingering in their collective consciousness, were taught that the role of wife and mother, keeper of that cozy hearth, was the last word in womanhood. Men's responsibilities, meanwhile, were all financial and work-related.

Nowadays, these roles seem rigid, unnatural, imprisoning, and downright deadly—but to our parents after the war, rules and roles and structure were a comfort. It wasn't until the late 1960s and early 1970s that women rebelled, saying no to being assigned one—lesser—role in life.

Now Nina has choices her mother would never have dreamed of. She has her own home, career, and sexual freedom. She is independent. She wants an equal relationship with a man—two independent people who are mutually supportive and equal. *Not* like her parents. God forbid, she'd rather stay single.

But Nina is still her mother's daughter. If she were, say, less demanding or less angry, she thinks she'd be better off. Unlike her mother, though, Nina doesn't really fall for this stuff—deep down, she knows it's a con. And in another way this daughter—and all of us who are daughters of traditional women—is quite unlike her mother. When Nina came to consult us about her relationship with Jack, we knew her at once as a woman just like ourselves. We know that you can be so good at taking care of yourself that you miss some important clues. When Jack won't go out of his way for her when she asks him to, Nina shrugs it off. But when she notices the same, repetitive pattern—an unwillingness to put himself out, or to think of *her* or *them* instead of *himself*—she doesn't want to think about it at first. Something she learned a long time ago wakes and whispers in her ear: *"I must be to blame."*

After we'd had a consultation with Nina, we urged her to come back—next time, with Jack. We had a hunch that Jack was a man in the middle—a Good Guy Today/Gone Tomorrow—far from hopeless, but definitely a guy who wants it all his way and expects a woman to pick up the slack. This couple was not on the same level of commitment. Even though they were monogamous, Jack chafed at responsibilities. Could he make the move from monogamy, Level Three, to Level Four, Monogamy Plus?

Before Nina and Jack came back for another session, Susan's image haunted us. One of us remembered all the times that she'd gotten up with the baby in the middle of the night because her husband was tired—never mind that she'd had a hard day, too. And the other remembered the time when she'd written her entire doctoral dissertation where her husband couldn't see her because she felt so guilty about the demands *her* work was placing on *him*. Since so many of the women who come to our offices are the same way, we did some serious thinking about why women kill themselves with responsibility.

Responsibility *does* have some crazy kinds of "benefits." If you're responsible for the relationship then it's under your control; this makes you feel powerful. The sad thing is that you aren't—you're the beast of burden; you lose sleep to protect him and you stand in your *own way* of getting things done (writing a doctoral dissertation in a closet won't help the cause).

So why do we keep doing it? Because it seems less painful than seeing that a man has to change. This makes anxiety well up inside us. Whether or not he changes is up to him, and we have a terrible feeling that he won't. This is too scary to think about. Instead, we ask: "What Did I Do Wrong?" or "How Can I Twist Myself into a Pretzel to Make Things Right?"

Meanwhile, the more responsibility *you* take, the less *he* takes. In *The Hearts of Men,* Barbara Ehrenreich talks about what she calls the male revolt—a male rebellion against the old bread-winner role that's ended in a male stance of almost total irresponsibility toward women. Meanwhile, women have become *overly* responsible.

What distresses us is the way so many therapists implicitly support this lousy state of affairs and, in fact, make matters worse. From some traditional therapists, Nina would hear that she had a neurotic tendency to choose "inappropriate" men and that she should undergo years of psychotherapy to uncover her "problem." The other stripe of traditional therapist (more couples-oriented) would advise her to back off and make fewer "demands" on Jack, so that he would want to pursue her. The message is: Accommodate! Don't expect too much from a guy if you want to "get" him. So therapists join with men in saying that women's desire for *more* is pathological. But why is it pathological for women to want *more* and not pathological for men to want *less?*

You've probably read a lot of books that say: Sure, the guy has problems—but you can't expect him to *change!* If anyone is going to change, Nina, it'll have to be you. This approach is toxic: because Nina is a woman, she is assumed to be the one who has more invested in the relationship and is more responsible for it. The therapeutic bias is clear: you can't expect very much from men (what a put-down of men!) so hands off the guy.

A woman like Nina needs total support in believing her demands are on the mark—and we try to give that support to our clients. Women *should* be making demands on men. If they don't, men will never change and never become equal partners in relationships.

Does Nina seek out "problem" men? No. The fact is that she could end up with three, four, or five Jacks in a row—and it still wouldn't be *her* fault. When we see so many Jacks, we'd be going against all the evidence if we believed that the Ninas of the world were choosing them. The plain fact is that *women are finding what's out there to be found.*

The "What Did I Do Wrong?" Syndrome

This syndrome has no useful purpose for women! Once a healthy woman thinks about it, she tells herself, "Wait a minute, I *didn't* do anything wrong." The way for any of us to tell how healthy we are is by noticing how long we cling to that first, knee-jerk response. But don't worry—even though you may think you're in an "I'm to blame" rut, most women will drop it and thankfully dust off their hands as soon as another woman, often a friend, challenges it.

Meanwhile, here are some typical ways the 1980s woman blames herself. You may have others to add to the list.

1. "I'm Too Demanding." When a man wants and asks for something from you, do you accuse him of being too demanding? No, he's just a confident, sexy guy who knows what he wants.

Laura fears she is being too demanding when she asks Jason what he does on the nights when he isn't with her. This question makes Jason feel "crowded," but, in fact, she isn't crowding him; she just wants to be close to him.

Jason grew up in a typical fifties family. His father (like Henry) was an overburdened man in a gray flannel suit who chafed at his responsibilities and resented relationships. Today's man wants a woman there when he wants her and gone when he's had enough—a desire that his father dreamed about, but rarely dared to expect.

Laura doesn't really think she's crowding Jason. They've been at Level Two, that of steady dating, but Laura has progressed to Level Three, monogamy, while leaving Jason behind; she's stopped seeing anyone else without knowing if the same is true for him. Another problem is that Jason hates to make plans in advance—even for the next weekend. Laura tells herself that Jason just likes to hang loose, or that he has lots of other interests. But sometimes, she has a flash that he is actually afraid of intimacy.

This awareness makes her cringe, so Laura sometimes tries to tell herself that Jason is right when he accuses her of being too demanding. If she agrees with him that their problems are *her* fault, she feels closer to him. At least they can agree on who is to blame! But this "close" feeling never lasts.

Laura has to realize that, for now, they are not on the same level of commitment. Jason is probably not ready to make the jump into monogamy and, realistically, Laura should think about dating other men (there's no sense in her being monogamous if she doesn't know that he is). But she can realistically demand that he plan dates with her in advance.

What *is* "too demanding"? If a woman expects a man to do everything *her* way, she is asking for too much. But quite frankly, this is rare; "making demands" is still "for men only." While women are beginning to get tougher, few are really comfortable with demanding enough. We try to help women find the "comfort level" for making demands, where it feels easy and natural.

Like many of us "demanding" women, Nina (whom we talked about earlier in this chapter) has high expectations of men and relationships. She is intense and fiery—she wants lots of affection, time, and energy from Jack. She also imagines the kind of involved, passionate relationship she wants. Realistically, she won't get it all. But the most important thing is her *wanting*—she is vital and alive! Why shouldn't she want an equal, intense, exciting relationship? Is there something wrong with wanting everything? We wouldn't squelch that part of ourselves, and we certainly would never advise you to.

It's okay to ask, it's okay to want, it's okay to stand up for what you want. Nina wants 100 percent more—*emotionally*—-from her relationship than her mother wanted from hers. The down side is that Nina will have more disappointments and frustrations than someone who doesn't want a lot—but she should never stop wanting.

Most of the time, though, when men tell women they are too demanding, all it means is that the woman wants more than the man wants to give. Men make women *feel* as if they're too demanding because men have a hair trigger about this issue. Again, for the man it's the fear of the loss of identity—the more he has to give to a woman, the more of himself he loses (or so he thinks). In our experience with couples, when a man tells a woman she's too demanding, he's really trying to get her to shut up. And it is *always* a show-stopper—a fast, easy way to bring a woman to her knees. And men know this. "I don't want him to think I'm desperate or shrewish," a woman thinks. "I guess I'd better put the lid on." Then, with the onus off himself, a man can breathe a sigh of relief.

Jack finds Nina too demanding even when what she wants is perfectly legitimate. "When a woman asks me for something, I freeze," he told us when he came to our office with Nina for a session. "It's just my nature."

"It's pretty crazy," we said, "to consider anything Nina asks for as a demand. You'll never give her anything she wants because your reaction will always be, 'No way; if she asks for it, I won't give it to her!' Of course, if she shuts up, she certainly won't get what she wants. What a catch-22 for Nina!"

Jack looked thoughtful. "I know there's something funny about it," he says. "The minute she wants something from me, I don't want to give it. It's perverse."

Jack *could* turn out to be perverse enough not to want to change, but it was definitely a good sign that he could take in what we had to say without denying it outright.

A man won't stop saying "You're too demanding" once you're married; then it's called "You're always nagging me." A married couple will make certain agreements about housekeeping, cooking, and shopping. Promises, promises! Then, he doesn't live up to his end (he wants *you* to do it all), and you remind him. He retorts with, "You're always on my back!" It's another catch-22. If you don't say anything, your guts churn inside you. If you do say something, he'll be sure to balk.

2. *"I'm Too Aggressive."* "Don't you think you're too aggressive?" one woman was asked by a friend after she and her husband had had a fight. "Sure, I'm aggressive—so what?" she replied. Call this woman aggressive, intimidating, overbearing, domineering, or whatever pejorative term you can come up with. She's just a normal woman with good, healthy, assertive instincts—she fights when she gets mad.

Judy's boyfriend, Frank, goes to pharmacy school by day and studies in the evening. Before he goes to bed, he calls her—it's a treat for him. But Judy needs lots of sleep; if she wants to talk to Frank, she has to prop her eyelids open with toothpicks. She's starting to get angry—he does everything he wants at his convenience, and she works hard all day, too! But she says nothing because Frank is "sensitive," and she doesn't want to hurt his feelings. Also, what if she says something, and he decides she's "too pushy"?

Being passive just won't work, and it isn't your job to protect a man's ego anyway. Judy, who is strong and assertive in every other aspect of her life, will blow up. Before it's too late (a little thing like this can get out of hand, fast), she should say to Frank, "Look, this late-night calling doesn't work for me. I love to talk to you, so let's figure out some better time." Frank may be sensitive, but he'll survive. In fact, when you set your own terms in a relationship, it makes both of you tougher. A Good-Enough Guy will be sure to rise to the challenge.

3. *"I'm Too Angry."*   When Nina blew up at Jack, he responded by telling her she was "an angry person." She was wiped out! Does it sometimes seem to you that a man has an uncanny knack for hitting your hot spots? We agree. Hearing that you're too angry makes you feel as if you're a downer, a negative person, and probably a man-hater. In any case, the implication is that you aren't *feminine.* Does he know what he's doing to you? No—he may be trying to defend himself. He isn't telling you that you are "an angry person" in order to break your back—he just wants to get you off *his* back.

The problem isn't your anger—it's that men hate you to be angry. As a child, a man may have felt terrified and overwhelmed when his mother was irked. Now, an angry woman shakes the foundations of his world. Unconsciously, a woman is probably tuned in to his need to be soothed, and her first instinct may be to *stop* shaking him up.

In sessions with couples, we find that when a woman acts hurt, she really is *angry.* The minute a woman starts crying, our antennae go up, and we suspect she's furious. We'll say, "Are you sad? We think it's something else." And it never fails that a woman will talk freely about her anger—all she needed was support.

When Nina gets angry at Jack for not being emotionally supportive of her—for not giving her more—and for not considering her needs, she is experiencing the same deprivation and rage felt by millions of other women. Her rage—your rage—is justified. In our society it's okay for women to cry, but not to get mad. This state of affairs should make any normal, healthy woman see red.

Think of all the situations in the last few weeks in which you've felt sad or hurt—more than likely, your true emotion was anger. In one of our group therapy sessions, Lynn talked about how her boss was assigning himself commissions that should have gone to her. But she was so worried about blowing up and being called "an angry broad" and "letting all hell break loose" that she excused the guy. Interestingly, the men in the group urged her to confront him—"He's cheating you; sue him!"—while the women tried to figure out how to tell him off "nicely."

For women, *relationships* are central. Dr. Carol Gilligan of Harvard University found in her research with children that girls will usually quit playing a game if personal troubles start brewing, while boys will discontinue the game if someone breaks the rules. Lynn is still a little girl on the playground—she protects her relationship with her boss instead of calling a foul.

All of us in the group supported her anger ("He was never your friend," we said, "he's been screwing you out of money!"), and finally she wrote a scathing letter to her boss. We held a victory party for Lynn—her well-aimed, well-articulated anger brought her the results she wanted.

4. "*I Said the Wrong Thing in Bed . . . at Dinner . . . at the Party . . . on the Phone . . .*" Your saying the "wrong thing" will never be the cause of his cold feet.

When Nancy met Bill at a party, lights flashed, bells rang, the music soared. He had another engagement that night, he told her, but why didn't they leave together? In the taxi, they made out passionately all the way to Nancy's apartment building. "I've never felt this way before," she blurted out at one point. "Me neither," he said. "I'll call you tomorrow," he promised breathlessly, giving her one long, last lingering kiss.

She never heard from him again.

She'd blown it. She'd turned him off; she'd said the wrong thing. But how could she have turned him off? He'd been just as excited as she was.

A man meets you and is attracted—there is a rush of emotion and desire, a wild exhilaration, and a promise of pleasure and fulfillment. In your mind you may leapfrog over several levels of commitment and may even imagine yourself sending out the wedding invitations! For you this is just the beginning; for him, it's the end. So many feelings have been aroused in him that his fear of engulfment button is pushed, and he takes off. To say this guy is Good For Nothing is putting it mildly—his life is most likely one quick fix after another. We see this happening again and again to women clients; even if it happens to you more than once, it's *not* your fault.

At the beginning of their relationship, Don would call Deirdre on Monday nights to make plans for the following Saturday. Then, one week he just didn't get around to calling till Thursday. The next week he didn't call at all, and the week after that, he waited till Thursday again. Deirdre thought she was losing her mind. "Is something wrong?" she asked. "Did I do something?"

Don wanted to feel that all his "options" were open. "I *want* to call her" had become "I *have* to call her": a duty. To the guy with cold feet, *any* routine, even one he likes, eventually becomes a burden. His fear of loss of identity (giving up pieces of himself) has raised its ugly head, and a woman should face the fact that he is probably lagging behind her on the levels of commitment. When this man feels that he "has to" or "should" do something for a woman, the ghost of his father rises in him—the man who spent his whole life "enslaved" by a wife and family. "I won't turn into my father," he vows to himself.

And basically, he feels entitled *not* to. In Don's father's day, "commitment," i.e., marriage, was assumed; it was the touchstone of adult status for men. Now a man may consider it his *right* to stay unmarried, unobligated, uncommitted for as long as it suits him. Since the breadwinner ethic has become outdated, we're seeing now how difficult it is for the new kind of "commitment" to take hold and a new kind of relationship to be born.

Don is a typical Good Guy Today/Gone Tomorrow. He is torn between an ideal of "freedom" and a desire to be close to Deirdre. She should watch what he does. She can experiment: if she says to him, "Fine, don't call me," or if she suggests that they take turns calling one another, do his feet get even colder? Deirdre only sabotages herself by thinking that she said or did the "wrong" thing. She needs to ask herself, "What does his response tell me about him? Why did calling me on Monday night trigger such a crazy reaction?" There is no "right thing" to say that will cure Don's, Jack's, or any other man's fears overnight. They had cold feet long before they met Deirdre or Nina—there is no magic cure for it, but it can help *immensely* to see his behavior clearly and not blame yourself.

5. *"I'm Not Sexy Enough."* Eve has brown hair, high cheekbones, and full, sensual lips. She couldn't be more beautiful and desirable—to everyone except her lover, Bill. Bill's "perfect woman" was dark, fiery, and Spanish, and the only time he was happy with Eve was after she came back tanned from Florida vacations. "Then," she said, "I was *in,* at least until the tan faded."

Bill's attitude was that he had to keep shopping around because Eve wasn't sexy enough. (He'd been pampered by his parents; for them, it had been the "earth, the moon, and the son," so of course the son couldn't settle for less than the stars.) Early on in the relationship, Bill set the ground rules: he didn't want a commitment, but as Eve said, "He wanted all the goodies that went with a commitment, like my being there for him and fulfilling his needs."

Since their sexual relationship wasn't terrific, Eve blamed herself. She wasn't sexy enough—obviously. "It never occurred to me," she said, "that *he* had sexual problems. I thought that if I had the right shape and face, everything would be okay."

We told Eve that the minute she finds herself thinking she should change her shape or color, a light bulb should go off—red alert! If a man doesn't think you're "right" as you are, something is off. The fact is, even if Eve had turned into Bill's mythical Spanish *doña,* it wouldn't have worked—then he'd probably have decided he liked blondes! No woman will be hot enough or gorgeous enough for the man with cold feet because, in the words of one man, "There'll always be a more beautiful woman around the corner." Don't let a statement like this make you feel like a hag. This isn't your problem—it's his fear crying out, not his sex drive.

Bill was a Good For Nothing Guy you could smell a mile away. Eve sees that now. But back then, Bill touched a sensitive spot about her beauty and sexuality. She was vulnerable, and he knew it. One woman's boyfriend told her that her legs were too fat. "What *nerve!*" we told her. "How dare he talk about your legs! Do you criticize *his* flaws?" She laughed and said of course she didn't. Finding fault with your body is a way for a man to put you down and control you by making you feel like an odd woman out.

Sometimes, a man can be shocked into changing his behavior. One man told his girlfriend he thought she should have breast implantations. She said, "Fine, I'll do it, as soon as you look into penis augmentation." Once he got over his shock, he told her he realized that unless he was willing to go under the knife himself, he had no right to ask *her* to.

Women are unbelievably vulnerable and sensitive about their faces and bodies—and this is a major hot spot men seem to hit with unfailing accuracy. When Eve looks back on her relationship with Bill, she sees that the reason their sex life wasn't terrific was that, to him, sex with her equaled commitment. As you will see in chapter 4, once a man is involved with you, his sexual behavior may become *under*whelming, to say the least. And because he doesn't want to face his own fears and anxieties about commitment, he may pick on your legs or your breasts as a way out.

6. "I Expect Too Much."   Think of what you expect from your women friends: reassurance, support, dependability, *intimacy.* Why shouldn't you expect—and get—the same thing from a man?

When Oliver gets sick, Felicia is at his bedside with aspirin and chicken soup. When he has a bad day at work, she drops everything to listen and make him feel better. When *she* gets sick, she's lucky if she gets a phone call. She is always *there* for him— why can't he be there for her?

Should you ever "compromise" in a relationship? We strongly believe there are things worth giving up to get. For example, you don't always have to be right. Both of us can recall in the early years of our marriages going to the wall on every issue. Now we pick our battles more carefully, choosing things that really mean a lot. One question we ask ourselves frequently is, "Can I live without this?"

Felicia *shouldn't* live without the kind of emotional support she wants from Oliver; if he can't give it to her, she may have to give up on him. We usually find that "compromise" in a relationship means letting a man have his own way. Women don't have to compromise the way they did when the most important thing in a woman's life was getting married; then, if she didn't give him his way, she had to face the gruesome possibility of never getting married. Now women are strong enough to set their own terms for marriages, or to choose to remain single.

If you compromise for a bad relationship, you'll find yourself turning into someone you don't like. You don't even have the *hope* of a good relationship because you're tangled up in your bad one. But women are *not* desperate to get a man; today's women are desperate to have good relationships. Many popular advice books tell women not to look at a man too hard. Put on your rose-colored glasses—see? He isn't all *that* bad. If a man is alive and moving, grab him. So what if you have to turn yourself inside out to get him?

We will advise you to stomp all over those rose-colored glasses—too many women have been blinded by them. We say there's a world of difference between two people negotiating a give-and-take, mutually beneficial relationship and a woman who tries to tell herself that less is enough.

7. *"I'm Too Smart."* Marlene is supposed to leave her smarts at the office. Her boyfriend, Dennis, doesn't like to hear that her boss at the bank regularly singles her out for special praise. At parties, he doesn't want her to disagree with his opinions. "I'm for equality in relationships," he says without a trace of irony, "but women have to remember that the male ego is fragile."

Women have egos, too—what is happening to Marlene's when she stifles hers "for the sake of the relationship"?

"I'm happy you got the promotion, but when we go out with friends, it makes me look bad if you talk about it." If you are used to hearing statements like this, take the first part of the sentence—before the *but*—and throw it away. The first part is only to placate you; after the *but* come his true feelings.

Do you want to be with a man who wants you to be less than you are? If the two of you got married and had children, would he want your daughter to be less than she could be? Obviously, many men will feel threatened by your success at work. A Good Enough Guy may admit to you that he feels this way—but he will nail the problem down to his own insecurity, not to your brains. A Good For Nothing Guy will pick away at your successes—do you really need him around to belittle you?

8. "I'm Not a Real Woman." If you were, you'd know where his socks are. You'd cook for him once in a while. You'd jump at the chance to do all the housework, even though you knock yourself out all day at work. You're trying to be too perfect, being a busy, competent career woman by day and a supportive, nurturing, feminine woman in your "leisure" time. A woman with a career sometimes becomes concerned that she is sacrificing the "feminine" side of herself. This is another vulnerability to which a man can apply pressure.

Does he know where *your* socks are? Does he cook for you? Do you like housework any more than he does? A man needs nurturing—but so do you. Many women balk at giving up the nurturing role; they're afraid there will be nothing to put in its place, and that if they give it up, the relationship will fall apart.

It doesn't have to. Rachel, a busy public relations consultant, is married to Will; the couple has a three-year-old child named Jerry. A while ago, Rachel sank into a depression, then she and Will came to see us. Rachel, who felt guilty about the long hours she spent at work, thought she had to be the Perfect Mother to Jerry, as well as the Perfect Wife. We told her that both she and Bill needed to set limits for Jerry—a three year old shouldn't be a despot—and that Bill should take his share of the housework. The hard part for Rachel was that she felt she must be a wonderful mother, wife, and career woman. Which, of course, she is. She just didn't quite see it yet.

Rachel couldn't wait to stop blaming herself for not being perfect—when she got firm with Jerry, her depression lifted, and the couple went in and out of therapy in a couple of months. Will learned that his responsibility for child care was equal to Rachel's, and, together, the couple was able to make the changes. (One of the reasons that women need so much support for this is that they are constantly blasted by "advice" about how to get even better at handling job and relationship responsibilities all alone. An article in the *New York Times,* for example, told women how to be perfectly successful at home and at work, without once suggesting that men share the burden at home, without even *mentioning* the role of men, in fact.)

Why, for women, does *having* it all mean *doing* it all? Deep down, Rachel didn't really want to keep house and be a single parent to Jerry. She was just afraid that it was what "real women" did. In her mother's day, the perfect wife and mother did everything Rachel did—but she didn't have a career on top of that! Being a superwoman is a super scam as long as men opt out of equal responsibility.

Most women are perfectly well aware that "What Did I Do Wrong?" is the *wrong* question to ask. We were all trained to be good little girls, and, unfortunately, we keep hearing a familiar voice whispering the question in our ears. Nina hears her mother, Susan; you hear your own mother. Our task is to show Nina, and all the women who come to us and read our book, that this voice is *not theirs.* To dispel your mother's voice, you have to make a wrenching separation from her. In fact, today's women have to separate from their mothers in a way women have never had to before.

It's painful; if you have no other model to follow, you may feel as if you're left in a vacuum. And that's why women who want a lot from relationships need some good, tough support in asking for, doing, and getting what they want. We don't believe that therapists should be neutral. We're developing a new style in which we help women break old patterns and have new, better relationships with men. We challenge, support, advise, and suggest because this method *works*. Women need transitional models to carry them over the chasm. We're not—nor will we ever be—neutral!

The problems that single women face today are unique, and the choices are harder. "I don't want a Prince Charming," one woman client says. "I want a man I'm attracted to on all levels—sexual, intellectual, and emotional. I'm not being true to myself by being with a man I don't respect. In that case, I would rather be single." As women continue to get stronger and more objective about relationships, many are taking the position vis-à-vis marriage so many men have been taking: marriage means giving up *too much*. This is not an easy position for women to take, but we want women to want the best—and not settle for less.

Nina came back to see us with Jack. In that session, Nina told Jack she was irked about all the little things that kept adding up; it still fell to her to manage their social life and dinners together, and usually Jack insisted on doing things his way or not at all.

Jack sighed. "When you smile, you're so sweet and I love to look at you, but when you're angry, I want to run."

We all laughed at the idea that Jack had come to therapy because, secretly, he wanted to make Nina "sweet" again. Men hate it when women get mad at them, yet they hate women who are doormats! Women "should be" assertive, independent, successful—and sweet (to them) all the time. Jack was a living contradiction. Did he realize it? Not quite.

Nina pointed out to Jack that she always had dinner ready for him when he came to her place after working late. But while she'd been working on the big project, and had come home dead tired every night, he hadn't lifted a finger to help. "Don't you see?" she said, "that if I'm working, I'd like you to do the same thing for me?"

Jack thought it over. Should women take care of all the "petty" details of a relationship? He knew it was wrong, but it wasn't easy to admit it and accept that he couldn't always have all things his own way. Both people have to fine-tune a relationship. Jack wasn't used to that idea, and Nina knew it was what she wanted but wasn't sure how to get it.

A few moments later, Jack said, "If I were with a less independent, demanding woman, things would be easy—but boring."

Right before the end of the session, Jack took a deep breath, as if he were about to take a terrifying plunge. "Well, okay," he said, "if you work late, I'll make dinner."

Nina laughed. "It would be great if you made dinner all the time."

"Oh, come on!" he protested.

And we all laughed. But we had the feeling Jack thought that some responsibility might not be all *that* bad.

It was a good start.

There *are* men who can rise to a woman's challenge. In the next few chapters, we'll talk about the sexual and social anatomy of the man with cold feet.

If you find yourself asking any of the following questions, you are probably falling into the "What Did I Do Wrong?" Syndrome. Reexamine your relationship more objectively, focusing on his behavior as well as your own.

- Am I too demanding?
- Am I too aggressive?
- Am I too angry?
- Did I say the wrong thing, in bed . . . at dinner . . . at the party . . . on the phone?
- Am I sexy enough?
- Do I expect too much?
- Am I too smart?
- Am I a "real woman"?

4

Cold Feet, Hot Women

Jon shifts uncomfortably in his chair. "I've been seeing this really great woman," he says and stops.

A moment later, he continues. "The problem is . . . sex. When she gets excited, she screams." He stops again and looks embarrassed. "I don't like it," he adds.

"That's strange," we say, "because it sounds as if *she* likes it a lot. She must really enjoy having sex with you."

"Well, maybe," he says reluctantly. "I never thought of it that way, but I don't know. It was a real turnoff."

In his mind Jon had a vision of the way in which women are "supposed" to act during sex. If a woman didn't fit into his vision, he no longer found her attractive and could no longer enjoy making love with her.

Since Jon is a venture capitalist, it occurred to us to appeal to his good business sense. "If you structure a deal, and your original idea doesn't work, is that the end?" we asked. "Don't you then try to find another way to make everyone happy?"

At first Jon just laughed. Then he said, "Of course. There are always other options."

"If you can do it in business," we said, "you can do it in the bedroom. It's a highly transferable skill."

How does the story end? It can go in one of two ways.

The Sad Ending: The next time we see Jon he talks about Allison again. Now he is turned off because she was "too intense" at a party the other night as she explained to a group of people the ins and outs of hcr work with a city agency. We tell Jon that, once again, he has found fault with Allison for not fitting in with his vision of how a woman should be. It is the same thing he'd been talking about last week. Jon looks at us blankly and shakes his head.

The Happy Ending: Thinking it over, Jon likes the idea of sexual options; he understands that while Allison isn't going to become *his* particular version of a sexy woman, she is sexy in her own right. In fact, the real Allison proves to be more exciting than his fantasy of a quiet, accommodating woman who takes his cues in bed just as she does everywhere else. How can a fantasy possibly compete with a real woman who responds so passionately to him? Jon is able to meet this aggressive, independent woman on her own terms—sexual and otherwise.

A Good Enough Guy will love a sexy woman who tells him what she likes and lets him know she likes it. But many men will expect—at least at first—women to live up to their private fantasies. We've found that men with serious commitment problems want women who are sexually enthusiastic (as long as they don't make demands) and sexually responsive (as long as they don't respond in their own way). If a woman does respond the way she wants to (not the way he wants her to), this man may pull back. For him, if sex isn't entirely on his terms, he feels as if he isn't in control. (And his terms may be the opposite of Jon's; he might expect a woman to scream her head off—"All of my women go wild in bed"—and if she doesn't, *that* turns him off.) One man told us that he'd asked his girlfriend to act out his favorite fantasy, but it had been a complete disaster. He'd wanted her to come to his apartment wearing a black garter belt and stockings under her coat and then seduce him. What she'd done instead was outfit herself in black bra, slip, and underpants as well—*not* part of the fantasy. Suddenly, it was no good—a turnoff. As soon as she participated in the fantasy, he no longer had complete control and the fantasy was shattered. He couldn't even bear to see her again, he told us.

When a woman responds or participates in her own way, a man can't help knowing she is a *separate person,* and that what they experience together will be as much her show as it is his. We want to emphasize that even though most men have a fantasy, some men, like Jon (he actually chose the "happy" ending), give it up for real life.

But usually, it isn't easy for men to make this substitution. Dr. Ethel S. Person, a psychoanalyst and researcher, talks about the myth of the Omni-Available Woman. In this male fantasy, women, who are ready for sex as soon as a man snaps his fingers, exist only to please men in *exactly* the way men want. This myth is about power and control; when a man is very young, he is power-less before his mother. Now, through sexual fantasy, he turns this upside down: *he* is powerful; *he* is in control.

One married woman puts in her diaphragm every night be-cause her husband may want to have sex. It is a turn-on for him that she is always ready and available for his advances (whether or not she really feels like it). He is in control. The fantasy of domination is a twin to the fantasy of omni-availabil-ity. When Ethel Person asked men about their sexual fantasies, she found that substantial numbers of them fantasized about torturing a partner or forcing her to submit to sexual acts; women reported almost none of these fantasies. The connec-tion between sadistic sexual fantasies and difficulties with inti-macy are clear: The fear of intimacy, or the fear of a *woman's* power, makes some men want to dominate or control women.

Men's fantasies of power and control over women have deep roots. In the 1950s, many men complained about "frigid" wives. But women had made an unconscious pact with their husbands—by being sexually passive, they were making their men look good. A man could complain that his wife "just laid there" while seeing himself as an insatiable sexual stud. When he fantasized about his wife being sexier, sexy was on his terms: that she would "go down on him," for instance. During the 1950s, "nice girls" didn't do this; it was an unspeakable act. With the sexual revolution, "nice girls" did it and, even more important, wanted men to go down on *them*. Suddenly men got more than they bargained for.

It didn't occur to men that if women started liking sex, they would make sexual demands of their own. The major result of the sexual revolution today is that women are more comfortable with their bodies and with sex. They know what they like and what they don't like. A Good Enough Guy *enjoys* the fact that he doesn't have to worry about what gives a woman an orgasm; he wants and expects her to tell him. But many men have problems with women who know what they like and ask for it. It's the men who don't want to deal with women in their own right who are having trouble. To these men, sexual demands signal emotional demands, and suddenly women's sexual demands become overwhelming.

The single most distressing result that we're seeing in our practices is that for men with cold feet, emotional intimacy with a woman means that *sex gets worse*. Now that men have supposedly gotten what they want—sexually enthusiastic women— they're pulling back!

A man may withdraw sexually or may even become sadistic. Usually he isn't aware that he's holding out and putting a woman down, and the bedroom becomes the arena where issues of power and control are acted out.

The Women Men Hate to Love

Myth or fact: Men don't like "sexually aggressive" women. The truth is that today's typical man with cold feet is having a love/ hate affair with the "sexually aggressive" woman. This term is loaded with negative meaning: an aggressive woman is unnatural, unfeminine—she makes too much noise! If a woman is aggressive, it is her own fault if she scares men away. In our practices we see women who may be labeled sexually aggressive, but whom we call sexually *positive*—women who initiate sex and openly enjoy it.

Some women flourish sexually with many lovers, but we've found that for most women sexual freedom means having good sex in a good relationship (particularly in the Age of AIDS). At the same time, for men, sexual freedom has come to mean the opportunity to have multiple partners and to move easily from one woman to the next.

For men who are threatened by sexually and emotionally secure women it is easier and less scary to be moving targets instead of sitting ducks. And women who *are* sexually and emotionally secure often end up feeling that if they are *too* good sexually, a man will be overwhelmed.

We find that many women now are puzzled and distressed by what seems to be a male retreat from, or rejection of, sex. If a woman tells a man that she wants more touching and caressing, for example, a man may refuse or ignore her request. Let's say he's always been open and sensual in bed with her before now, but lately, they've been getting closer and spending more time together. Now, when she makes a sexual request, he feels as if she is trying to "take over." But as the strength of his connection with this woman has deepened, he has begun to feel that she is trying to "take over" in all areas of his life. In flight from her self-assertion, he may accuse her of being "too demanding," and initiate impersonal "fucking" sessions as a way to distance himself from her.

A man whose current girlfriend has just received a pay raise and promotion that puts her head and shoulders over him in the job market may punish her by withholding sex. It is *very likely* that he does not know he is doing this. Or, as one man told a woman client of ours, she was not "mediocre enough" for him. "I need someone I don't have to compete with," he blurted out to her. "I *don't* need someone who's all that terrific." At the same time, their sexual relationship became impersonal and perfunctory. The fact is, now that some women are financially and professionally successful, and men can no longer count on them being "mediocre" or "accommodating," the balance of power in many areas of relationships has shifted—and some men are using sex in a frantic attempt to recoup their "losses."

In their first session with us, Bill and Kate hinted at sexual problems; finally, we came out with a direct question: "How is your sex life?"

"Terrible!" Kate said immediately.

And then Bill told the story. When the two began editing a documentary film together, Bill knew at once that he'd never been so attracted to any woman before. Privately, he decided that not only was she just his type—small, dark-haired, and energetic—but also that her ideas were brilliant. He had to go out with her.

Kate was interested, too; she liked Bill's quiet intensity, and she had the feeling that once he became involved with a woman, he would become serious. They began seeing each other. A few months later, after Bill's roommate moved out, they decided they might as well pool their resources and live together. A month after Bill moved in with Kate, he began begging off sex—"I'd get turned off whenever she got turned on," he said. And he began to hate public displays of affection—"slobbering all over each other," he called it—when Kate only wanted to hold hands! Then Kate picked up the story. On the rare occasions when they did have sex, she said, it was "impersonal fucking," which she despised. She'd concluded that if he behaved this way, he must despise *her*.

A few sessions later, after we'd found that Bill was not only withdrawn sexually but in other ways, too (he'd practically stopped talking to Kate, and he constantly made dates to see his friends without including her), we suggested that he move out. Obviously, the couple had moved much too quickly to Level Five, living together, and now Bill was reacting to that by withholding

[75]

sex. A cautious return to Level Three, monogamy, made the most sense.

The two of them looked at us, then at each other. Bill swallowed nervously, and Kate pulled at the hair that was slipping out of a clip. Obviously, they didn't know whether to feel fearful or relieved. We then told them we thought they should continue to see one another, but that the combination of emotional and sexual intimacy had proven "too hot" for Bill. His natural instinct had been to cover himself by withdrawing sexually, but we didn't believe he'd consciously wanted to put Kate down or that he was terminally turned off. "I got myself in too deep," he'd said at one point, and that had been our clue. Kate was the woman he wanted, but when he got what he wanted, he got scared. We wanted to see if things would improve once Bill had some "space."

But Bill was shaking his head. "No, I can't believe that," he said. "It isn't something I'd do. I've never had sexual problems! I mean, I do think I moved in too soon; if my roommate hadn't left, I might have waited. Maybe Kate and I are on different timetables."

We felt that Bill was a Good Guy Today who might make it—not only did he *not* despise Kate, he was obviously in love with her. Now he was humiliated by the fact that their sex life had deteriorated. But we had the feeling that things might improve. "Give this relationship some time and space," we said. "Let's see what happens in the next few months."

What we heard later was that the night Bill moved out, he went out to the store, brought back some whipped cream, and initiated the best sex they'd had in months. Then, in the weeks after he left, both he and Kate became very sad and depressed. They missed one another's company and found it difficult to be apart for days at a time. But their sexual relationship continued to be good—sad as Bill was, when he knew he could leave Kate's bed for his own bed, his own space, his boundaries stayed intact. As long as Kate was somewhat distant and poignantly unavailable, she was no threat to his shaky sense of self.

Staying on Top

Until recently, the only "sexual problem" that would bring a man into therapy was impotence. What we're seeing now among our clients is a wholly different level of sexual problems that have to do with the way a man *interacts* sexually as opposed to how he functions or performs. Issues of power and control are at stake, as the man struggles to "stay on top" of the woman he's attracted to.

When Charles, who is a photographer in his early thirties, and Natasha, a teacher in her late twenties, first came to see us, we sensed immediately that the problems were deeper than they seemed to know. "When I first met her, Natasha was everything I wanted," Charles told us in our first session. "She's a motivated person, a real friend, and an attractive woman." But everything he described to us after that belied his words. The first night they slept together, Charles set up an elaborate seduction scene, with dinner, wine, and candlelight. He planned, he said, to "conquer" Natasha, but when she announced to him that she *wanted* to spend the night with him, Charles became disappointed—and angry. Why? If Natasha was ready and eager for sex, then he couldn't conquer her! With Natasha a willing participant in her own seduction, the thrill was gone.

After this inauspicious beginning, Charles stepped up his demands on Natasha: he wanted her to be completely passive in bed so that his most aggressive fantasies could come into play, and if she ever dared to tell him what *she* wanted, he became furious. Natasha hated these routines, and the only reason she stayed with Charles, she said, was that they were such good companions in other ways. A fiercely determined woman who hated to give up on anything she started, she was willing to fight for the relationship. But she was baffled by his sexual behavior— on that fateful first night, she'd simply assumed he wanted her to participate. Until then, he'd given every indication that he was "liberated" and actually liked "aggressive" women, and that he'd wanted what she considered to be an equal, participatory sexual relationship.

Charles always had the feeling, he told us, that he was incapable of having a good relationship with a woman. He was used to feeling isolated and lonely, but when he met Natasha, whom he'd seen as his "perfect" woman, he'd wanted to prove to himself that he could have a relationship. Immediately, though, he'd found himself frantically trying to "master" her—if he didn't, she might prove too much for him.

This was a clear impasse, so we gave them a firm injunction: "No sex." We felt it was important for them to have a fresh start.

But Charles's problems were so serious that even a rest from sex did not dispel his fears and fantasies. Out of desperation, Natasha devised an unsatisfactory "compromise" in which Charles could watch a pornographic movie on the VCR while they were having sex; by keeping himself once removed from Natasha, he didn't feel so threatened that she would overpower and consume him.

You might think that it would be difficult for us to feel sympathetic to a man whose main sexual fantasy is to tie up and humiliate the woman he supposedly loves. What helps us be empathetic is learning about what makes a man who he is. Charles's father was an incorrigible bully who lorded it over his meek, agoraphobic wife. Charles loathed his father for his disgusting behavior but at the same time joined him in disdain for his mother. Charles learned from his father that maleness meant ruthless aggression against women. As an adult, though, he tried to break the pattern by choosing a woman—Natasha—who, as an independent career woman, couldn't have been more unlike his mother. The problem, then, was that he needed to make Natasha just as helpless as his mother.

Charles's anxieties went far beyond the bedroom. His real fear was that he would become weak and dependent on Natasha. Many men secretly wonder if women who are financially and professionally successful will actually prove to be *more* successful, competent, and powerful than they are. This fear makes some men feel too small, too weak, too incompetent. Frantically, they try to make themselves feel strong, but this "strength" can't really fool anyone; inside, a man like Charles is terrified.

Natasha had to decide whether to keep fighting for the relationship, or to leave. We knew that making this decision was keeping her awake at night; she'd come to therapy with dark circles under her eyes and she'd lost weight. We sensed that she wished we'd make the decision for her, and finally one day, in a phone call, she asked us in a tearful, shaking voice what she should do. We explained to her as gently as possible that we couldn't tell her. "The purpose of therapy," we said, "is to give you enough information to make your own decision. It seems to us now that you have all the information you need."

She waited, as if we might say more. But we didn't because we could tell she wasn't yet ready to give up.

Six months later, we heard from Natasha again. She'd become convinced, on her own, that nothing short of total submission to Charles was the price she'd have to pay for the relationship. The price was too high, and she left him.

We're always hopeful that once a woman has the right information, she will be able to identify a bad risk and get away as fast as she can. This is even more important now, when a man's need to keep a sexual upper hand can actually come down to a matter of life and death. To forget that we're living in a time when sex can literally kill you is too dangerous.

Because she knew that Jake had an active sex life, Sara decided to ask him to start using condoms when they had sex. Jake scoffed at Sara's request. Only wimps wore condoms, he told her. And besides, he got a sexual rush from the possibility that he might make her pregnant. But when Sarah insisted, he told her she was being castrating. That stung her; for a moment she wondered if she was. But no, she wouldn't fall for it. He was only trying to make her take the rap.

That night, as soon as they got into bed, Sara handed Jake the condom. Jake turned away and fell asleep. The following morning he asked her to go down on him, just for a moment, and then surprised her by ejaculating into her mouth. Frustrated and furious, Sara realized Jake had used every sneaky way he could to get out of using a condom. What bothered her almost as much as the threat of disease was Jake's total disregard for her wishes. Even if he'd thought her fears were entirely unfounded, he'd shown her that, in his book, his pleasure was all that counted. Jake is strictly Good For Nothing.

In the Age of AIDS, every woman should bring condoms along when she thinks she will be having sex with a man whose sexual habits and history are not well known to her. Since for many men sexual freedom has meant multiple partners, *it is critical* for a woman to be realistic. A new lover may have had any number of encounters in his past, and by sleeping with him you are in a sense sleeping with all of them. For this reason, *any man who refuses to wear a condom is Good For Nothing.* Period. There are no excuses. Either he won't do it because *you* are asking him to do it (thinks you're "too demanding" or doesn't like to feel "obligated" to do anything for you) or he's convinced he is too tough for anything to happen to him.

For him, an agreement to use a condom means that he has "given in" to you, and that you are controlling the sexual game; for him, sex *is* a game—a power play. Maintaining his myth of toughness is far more important to him than safeguarding your health. Also, remember that many men associate AIDS with homosexuality. Your request for a condom may spark latent fears and doubts he may harbor about his manhood. If it's a question of your life or his ego, your choice is obvious.

The sexual revolution is over for everyone—and men are just beginning to catch on. But this won't be easy. For men, it means giving up the old fantasy of the Omni-Available Woman. In the 1950s it was strictly a fantasy, and if a man acted it out at all, his partner was a "bad" woman. With the sexual revolution, the sons of these men were given full license to pursue what has been the most vividly imagined, achingly yearned for dream of men everywhere. One man said: "In my fantasies, I'm a whoremaster, with bevies of gorgeous women clamoring for my attention." In real life, this man is happily married and completely faithful! And another happily married Good Enough Guy, who willingly traded sleeping around for security, love, and continuity but who still gets nostalgic when he recalls the good old days, said: "It isn't any one woman I'm hungry for, it's the idea that I could have sex with any number of women any time I wanted."

But now more and more men are running into women who say "Forget it" to casual sex. Women have moved beyond the sexual revolution to the *relationship* revolution. It isn't as flashy, but it's the next phase—and there's no going back.

The Sexual Minefield

During sex, people experience their boundaries dissolving. A Good Enough Guy knows this is temporary; for other men, however, sex becomes the natural place for fear to take over. Fortunately, most men are not as severely phobic as Charles or Jake; what you are most likely to find is ambivalence. With many men, there are ways to handle this. Now we're going to discuss a whole range of bed behavior that can tell you where a man stands on the commitment-fearing spectrum.

If a man wants to have sex and you don't, he may try to convince you that your sex drive is "too low." Walter wants to have sex every night and since his wife, Sally, doesn't, Walter tells her she isn't as highly sexed as she should be (she isn't "sexy enough"). He assumes that it's fine for him to relieve tension through sex; he also assumes that Sally will like what he likes.

Finally, Sally rebelled; she'd felt *obligated* to have sex and sometimes, now, she hated it. Angrily, she told Walter she thought he could just as well masturbate.

Amazed, Walter said, "Wouldn't you rather have sex with me than have me masturbate?"

"No," she said. "At least not the way things are now."

When Walter thought about it, he realized that what was good for him was terrible for Sally. "Well, it isn't my first choice," he said in answer to her suggestion, "but okay—I guess."

Once Sally had jumped out of the sexual pressure cooker, she began to want to have sex again. She began to initiate it herself. For the first time, the couple began to learn and appreciate one another's minds and bodies. A Good Enough Guy, like Walter, may assume that your needs are the same as his, and he probably will not realize at first that you are not obligated either to fulfill all his needs or feel the same way he does. However, when confronted, he'll probably realize he's out of line.

Unlike Walter, a real Good For Nothing Guy will use sex to relieve his tensions without regard for your feelings. He thinks that sex on demand is his right. He harasses you when you don't want to and makes you feel guilty. He digs in his heels and refuses to negotiate. But many men, after an initial resistance, *will* negotiate.

Now that women have become more openly sexual, a man with cold feet may respond to a woman by telling her she is too demanding. Ask a man for "foreplay" and see what happens. We've heard a lot about reluctance and outright refusals. You may tell him that you really want oral sex and he won't try, or he may want oral sex and never reciprocate. It's also common for men to balk when a woman suggests a new sexual position. "I thought we'd settled that," one man said when his girlfriend suggested they try sex standing up. For this man, exploring new ways to experience sexual pleasure is a threat. If *you* suggest it, he fears loss of control. He isn't really a prude, but he is afraid of engulfment—too many good feelings with one woman may equal too much involvement.

This same man may also resist when you try to guide his hand in a way that you know gives you pleasure—again, he fears loss of control. If you tell him what to do, he doesn't feel powerful. He may also refuse to discuss sex with you, or accuse you of "breaking the mood" if you want to. He'll sulk and claim that you "blew it." Apparently, everything was perfectly magical until you opened your mouth.

If, like most women, you've had at least one of these experiences with a man, the first thing to remember is that it is *his* problem—not yours. Second, take a good, objective look at him. Is this specific sexual behavior typical of him? If you want to go to a particular movie or eat Chinese food, does he refuse simply because *you* suggested it? Does he have to have everything *his* way? If so, for this man, *everything* is a power struggle, and you may have to consider him hopeless.

It is equally important to remember, however, that even Good Enough Guys have lots of difficulties with sex and intimacy. None of the behavior that we've just described automatically eliminates a man. One man, who at first refused to perform oral sex on his wife because he "couldn't stand the taste," later learned to enjoy kissing her thighs while massaging her clitoris with his fingers until she had an orgasm. For her, this was a wonderful, loving compromise—a sign that he cared about what made her feel good. In another couple, the wife wanted sex more often than her husband did. At first shy about asking—would he think she was "too demanding"? she finally told him she wasn't satisfied. Together, they worked out manual and oral ways to satisfy her without intercourse.

You must always be clear and straightforward with a man about what you want because this is an excellent way to find out any number of important things you need to know about him. Can he talk with you about sex? Does he get angry—and stay angry—at you if you try to talk about it? Or can he get over his anger, look inside himself, and discover the source of his own fears?

A man *will not* initiate change by himself. You can choose to placate his fears and stifle your own needs. But why should one person in the relationship be unhappy? And why should that one person be you? If you persist in talking with him about sex and letting him know what you want, you may find that eventually he responds.

How long should you try? This is tricky because individuals take varying amounts of time to change. Don't, for example, expect the man who won't try new positions to turn into a sexual tiger overnight. But if you have tried for, say, three months to change the situation and have made no progress, forget it. If you have made some progress, wait and see if it continues, but always put a time limit on it.

The New Impotence

A Good Enough Guy will want to arouse a woman. He will be eager to try new positions that you suggest—in fact, he'll love it! Even if he is reluctant at first (he'll probably be a little intimidated), he won't accuse you of pressuring him or being too aggressive when you make your wishes known.

However, the idea—or threat—of sex and intimacy in the same place at the same time with the same woman can turn even the best guys into temporary sexual basket cases. When they meet women to whom they're deeply attracted, they frequently act in ways that perplex and put off the women they want. In fact, these men in love so often show a particular kind of sexual behavior that we're convinced it's a trend in itself.

Paul, a salesman in his early thirties, moved in with Holly, a teacher, 36. After the move, Paul became impotent. At first, he tried to blame Holly. She was slightly overweight, and he told her he'd find her more attractive if she took off a few pounds. But in his heart Paul knew his impotence was not Holly's problem; he was well aware of his own fears. This was the first time he'd gotten close to a woman; a former alcoholic, Paul had been alone for several years. Now he had fallen in love with a warm, affectionate, intelligent woman who wanted to share her home with him. Paul was overwhelmed; setting up sexual barriers was a way for him to define his personal boundaries.

At first, Holly had been crushed when Paul lashed out at her. She'd always been sensitive about her weight, yet she thought of herself as an attractive, sexual woman. But apparently Paul was turned off by her. Then she got mad. He'd never been turned off before now! So what was the *real* problem?

Meanwhile, Paul had decided to talk with Holly about his fears. He didn't have enough space of his own in her apartment, he told her, and he felt crowded by all of her possessions. Holly readily agreed to clean out a room for him that would serve as his den, and she also made sure that he had plenty of closet space. Then they shopped together for some new furniture, and gradually Paul felt more at home. The apartment was no longer hers—it was *theirs*. Over the course of time, his impotence vanished.

When Jim met Roberta at a dinner party, he fell in love at once. He was embarrassed to tell anyone, much less Roberta. After all, here he was, 44, and divorced with two children. He wasn't young, and he certainly was no longer romantic, if he ever had been. In fact, he'd become cynical; there'd been the bad marriage, and then other, futile affairs that hadn't gone anywhere. But Roberta, over ten years younger than he was, aroused in him feelings he never knew he had. He was as tongue-tied as a teenager when he asked for her phone number, and was genuinely amazed when she agreed to go out with him.

Two months later, they were seeing one another regularly, and Jim was feeling increasingly ardent. But he could not bring himself to make a sexual move—he was terrified that she'd laugh him off, or that they would go to bed and she would find him a washout. And anyway, he wanted to wait for a sexual signal from her. The last thing he wanted to do was press her to have sex with him if she didn't want to. So he waited—in agony.

Finally, one day while they were out for dinner, Roberta said, with a slightly exasperated smile, "Well, Jim, are you *ever* going to take me to bed?"

Jim reacted with a mixture of delight, relief, and shame—what an idiot he'd been for waiting! But now, thank God, the waiting was over. However, as they left the restaurant together for Roberta's apartment, he was sweating and his heart was pounding. If he'd ever had cold feet, it was now.

Even as he climbed into bed and gathered Roberta close, he couldn't dispel the fear. "Oh, God," he thought despairingly, "what is *wrong* with me?" And in fact, Jim was impotent that night. But Roberta was great—she didn't panic, get mad, laugh, or tell him to get lost. She kissed him and brought them some wine from the kitchen; then together, the two of them found other ways to satisfy her. After they'd gone to bed a few times, Jim's impotence disappeared, and he turned out to be a great lover.

A Good Enough Guy like Jim usually won't try to seduce or conquer a woman; in fact, he will show a genuine respect for the woman's right to decide if and when the couple has sex. For this man, the bedroom is not the battleground—he is secure enough to let a woman be a full sexual participant and to share the control. After his initial anxiety wears off, his sexual problems usually prove to be temporary.

About six months after Bill moved out of Kate's apartment, he came to see us privately for an update. He and Kate had just returned from a vacation in Jamaica. In the months since we'd seen them, they'd spend a lot of time together, and there'd been no repetition of the sexual problems that had brought them into therapy; sex, in fact, had been great. (Level Three, monogamy, was perfect for them at this point.) Once they were in Jamaica, however, everything was fine *except* for sex. Each night, after being together all day and feeling close and loving toward one another, Bill would fall into bed and be sound asleep before Kate had finished taking a shower. Or else he would fall asleep watching TV . . . or else he would suddenly want to take a walk by himself on the beach. . . .

After a few days Kate began asking what was wrong. "We're closer than we've ever been before," she said. "We should be *living* in bed. Why aren't we?"

At first Bill didn't want to think about it. "I'm just tired," he told her. "I'm trying to relax and cool out. I can't just come down from the work week overnight."

But as a few more days went by with no change, Bill began to remember what we'd talked about in therapy months before: that when they were the closest, he felt the least like having sex; that when things got too good between them, he had to pull back. When he and Kate were alone here on the island, there was no escaping the double bed they shared—there was *nowhere to run*. Just the thought of it made anxiety well up inside him: he wanted to have sex with Kate, and yet he still needed to keep to himself.

Then at some point he suddenly remembered how he'd felt as a child when his parents divorced; he'd never been able to trust intimate relationships since then. So was he going to blow this relationship with Kate? Would he allow old traumas to shape his present life and his future? Bill prided himself on having control over his life, doing and getting what he wanted; he became severely uncomfortable with the idea that he was allowing other forces—his own fear, mainly—to control him. He resolved to bring the subject up with Kate next day.

"I don't think I'm falling asleep early just because I'm tired," he told her. "I think it's more complicated than that."

At first, Kate was impatient. Gesturing around them at the beautiful red and orange sunset, the palm trees, the glowing white sand, the bougainvillea vines hanging from the trellis, she said, "Look, I think I understand. But you're wrecking this great vacation!"

Bill said, "I've never been on vacation with a woman before. We're together on this island; I can't get away!" They both laughed, and Bill had the feeling that a barrier between them had been broken.

"You are really crazy," Kate said. "And you've got twenty-four hours to get over it!"

When Bill noticed how beautiful Kate looked in the island light, he had the feeling that twenty-four hours would be more than enough.

Sexual signals that disguise problems with commitment include:

- As your relationship becomes more intimate, sex gets worse instead of better.
- He loses interest in sex after a move toward more intimacy in the relationship.
- He begins to change his style of lovemaking; where before he was sensitive and gentle, now he goes for "rough" sex or stimulation through hard-core pornography.
- He wants you to be entirely passive in bed so that he can play out his fantasies on you; if you make suggestions or take any part in the fantasy, you "ruin" it for him.
- He refuses to use a condom despite your intention to practice safe sex.
- He has no interest in foreplay and ignores your specific requests for kissing and caressing before intercourse.
- You go on a vacation and the more time you spend together the less interest in sex he has; you, however, feel closer to him than ever before.

5

Psyching Out Cold Feet

"When a woman asks me for something, I freeze . . ." "I put up walls, I don't know why . . ." "I'm not threatened by her, I just don't listen to her . . ." "When she nags me, I turn a switch to OFF . . ."

We hear these statements—and more just like them—again and again, in therapy sessions, workshops, and seminars, at dinner parties and in casual conversations, from men who are stockbrokers and investment bankers, doctors, sex therapists, artists, and academicians. When we first began conducting our clinical research, we thought that intimacy was a problem for just a few troubled men. But the fact is that *all* men in our society smell danger in intimate relationships with women, at least to some degree. For many, the first, most elemental response is to withdraw.

"There can only be one person in charge, and that person has to be me!" "I need to be the man of the house." "I don't care if a woman is aggressive at work, but *not* at home." As the men who withdraw do, these men smell danger, too, and their response is to *control* or *dominate.*

But while men experience danger in relationships, they are rarely aware that fear is the fuel they're running on. Instead, they perceive danger lurking "out there" in intimate relationships with women. Carol Gilligan, a research psychologist, found that for men and women, red flag alerts go up at different times. For men, danger lurks in intimate contexts, while women sense it in more impersonal, competitive situations. Gilligan used a test in which a subject is asked to interpret drawings of vague, ambiguous social scenarios. In interpreting the pictures, a person will see his or her own conflicts and problems. A man who has no idea that he fears intimacy will project onto a picture of a couple sitting together on a park bench a scary, violent story. In Gilligan's sampling, 21 percent of eighty-eight responding men did just that, telling, among other things, stories about "entrapment" and "smothering relationships." None of the fifty women in her study sensed danger in this scene; nor did any woman write a violent story about the same picture.

Men's sense of danger in intimacy has its source in early childhood. We have found that even when a man agrees intellectually that his fear of intimacy is irrational and that he behaves destructively toward women, his fears stay as strong as ever. (His behavior *can* change, however, once he understands what he feels.) Unquestionably, a hidden wellspring of primal feelings continuously (and unconsciously) shapes the responses of all adult men to women and to intimacy.

We depart from the bulk of traditional developmental literature, which is slanted toward one basic idea: that castration anxiety is the major motif of a man's identity and that the Oedipal period, the time when he becomes consciously "different" from little girls, is the central event in his psychological development. According to the Oedipal theory, maleness emerges through a three-year-old boy's "love affair" with his mother (his closeness with her becomes sexualized) and competition with his father for the mother's love. But the little boy is terrified that his father will become enraged and cut off his penis as punishment for trying to take Mother away. This is such a nightmare that the boy *identifies* with his father rather than competing with him, at the same time rejecting intimacy with his mother. Sadly, from the age of three on, a little boy has only his father, most likely a remote, inaccessible figure, with whom to identify.

But as far as we're concerned, Oedipus has a long way to go in explaining the sorts of problems we see men having with intimacy! Our suspicion is that it is only part of the truth and that the differences between boys and girls begin much earlier and go much deeper.

There exists now a new wave of theorists—primarily women—who are building an object relations theory with respect to male and female differences. Their names are not yet household words. Their voices are different and exciting, although their work has been ambivalently received by the classical community. This cutting edge of psychological theory grew out of feminism and combines cultural analysis with psychology. What is "male"? What is "female"? These theorists come up with some new answers.

Along with Carol Gilligan, Nancy Chodorow, Lillian Rubin, and Dorothy Dinnerstein have taken the examination of sex differences beyond the Oedipal stage into the even murkier depths of the preverbal—or pre-Oedipal—period in human development. This is the time between birth and the third year of life in which your world is all chaotic sensation and raw, visceral feeling. You are at your most primitive level of need, and, depending on whether or not those needs are met, your world view is taking shape.

Whether we are female or male, we all start out adoring closeness; babies love to be held and cuddled, and, in fact, all the baby knows is a paradise of union. In this symbiotic state, a baby feels as if it is literally one with the person who holds it, feeds it, and loves it. Then, at about six months, as a result of a physiological thrust toward separateness, the infant begins slowly to become aware of a world beyond Mother, as well as the fact that it is different and separate from her. The baby is beginning to develop its own ego boundaries, which it must do in order to evolve as an individual.

During the pre-Oedipal period the baby internalizes the world by resolving it into mental images. The child forms an image for each important person, incorporating each image into a personal point of view. As an adult, the primitive images of those people still hold—and so do the feelings. If you are a boy and your primary caretaker is a woman, this primal experience with a woman will be the litmus test for your response to all women.

It has been taken for granted that if a mother and child, specifically a son, get along well during these first three years of the child's life, the outlook for his future is happy and healthy. Naturally, it makes sense that a good relationship with his mother will benefit a man in later life. But on another level there is something very wrong with a few basic assumptions here. First of all, traditional literature has glorified and idealized the mother-child bond, making it into a Madonna fantasy of perfect union. The fact is that this sacred niche is fraught with danger for the woman because she has *all* the responsibility. There are a thousand and one ways for a woman to louse up her child, and since most of the time she is the only adult involved, she's been set up to fall short.

And the mother isn't the only one to lose out. Even if the mother-son relationship is as good as it can get, the implications for the boy's future are bleak. The single most destructive event in the lives of today's men is really a *non-*event—the absence of their fathers from the shaping of their emotional lives. And with fathers not involved in child-rearing, women are left as the hated and adored All-Powerful Parent, an almost mythologically pro-portioned figure capable of giving and withholding love. To the young boy, his mother wields lightning bolts of absolute power and control: she is the first person to say "no," the one who insists that he give up diapers, who tells him to eat his peas, who de-mands that he behave at the table, wear a hat when it's cold outside, and go to bed before he wants to. She is squelching his spirit! The boy never forgets that a *woman* did this to him, so it's easy to see why so many men feel they must *control* women—in his earliest experience, a woman controlled him, and if he isn't careful he will become a baby again.

A man who, in adult life, needs to control women is unconsciously reenacting a time when his mother was strong and he wasn't. A Good For Nothing Guy, who needs to dominate you, is replaying his relationship with his mother, only this time he's the bigger, stronger player. The Good Guy Today/Gone Tomorrow overreacts to the issue of control by jealously guarding his freedom. The Good Enough Guy may *wish* he could have it all his way in a relationship, but when he's challenged by a woman, will come around to see that she does not exist to serve him.

Margaret Mahler, an expert on the separation process between children and their mothers, describes a tortuous period in the small child's life that she calls rapprochement. At this point, the child is between eighteen and twenty-four months old. During this period, the male child begins to wrench himself away from his mother and go out into the world. Repetitively, he leaves and comes back for some more of the "good stuff"—the old, blissful closeness with his mother. Then, jolted out of the dream by the fear of losing himself, he tears himself away. When he gets enough "distance," the fear of being without his mother brings him back to her for "refueling." He continues this seesaw—staying close and moving away—until he feels safe and confident on his own.

Meanwhile, the boy is becoming aware of his genitals and beginning to define himself as male. Unfortunately, since the primary person from whom he is separating is Mother (woman) instead of Parent (woman *or* man), the boy's entire concept of what it means to be male is focused on *not being like her.* Closeness and intimacy are entirely associated with her, woman; therefore, in order to become a separate individual *and* a man, he must not only reject his mother but reject intimacy, too.

The parallel experience for a girl doesn't hurt so much—she can be close to her mother even *while* she's separating and developing a gender identity. In adult life, a woman is likely to be more comfortable with reciprocity in a relationship, while a man is more likely to want to take without giving anything back. One of the reasons that so many men want women to *take care of them* is that they yearn unconsciously to go back to that time of complete indulgence, pre-rapprochement.

It is both easier and harder for boys to separate from their mothers than it is for girls. Easier because sexual difference is visible, tangible evidence that mother and son are separate individuals. Harder because boys have to "give up" their mothers to solidify a male identity and also because separation, spurred on because the boy has different genitals than the mother, is a *false reason* to separate. If both parents are primary, a boy would still have to separate in order to grow, but he would *not* be forced to reject women and closeness in order to do so.

It is something like death at an early age. Pieces of a boy's psyche may be killed off, stunted, or badly damaged. He may grow up "male," but he does *not* grow up a whole person, with a full, flourishing capacity for mutual love. In fact, no matter how good enough a guy may be as an adult, he may still feel that closeness to a woman means losing pieces of himself.

A client of ours, Phil, told us of a strange, dreamlike experience he'd had one night while he was at the theater with his girlfriend, Regina. Before the play began, Phil wanted to hobnob with friends of his in the theater lobby; Regina had had a bad day at work and wanted him to be alone with her for a few minutes in the quiet, more isolated anteroom of the theater. When Phil looked into the anteroom where Regina sat waiting for him, he was struck by the darkness of the room and the sense that he would suffocate if he went inside.

When Phil free-associated to the image of the anteroom, he spoke of a sense of "smothering" and "envelopment," of being drawn into the dark, close place so powerfully that he couldn't resist, and that if he gave way, he would be obliterated. When Phil told us this, he laughed—part of him knows that a theater lobby is hardly this scary—and he understood that he was actually expressing his fear of involvement with Regina. Phil is a guy who is aware of his fears; even so, old feelings have a life of their own.

For Phil, the notion of intimacy between himself and Regina shook loose from his unconscious the memory of his early, fearsome and blissful union with his mother.

Phil's experience is typically male and not at all unusual—nor is he in any way incapable of intimacy. Because he can read himself pretty well, he has some control over his behavior. For many men, feelings they had as three year olds are not so easily talked about. A man may repetitively get close to you and drop out of your life. He blames *you* for his behavior—"You're too demanding" or "You're not sexy enough" become the "reasons" for his conflict. Some men believe this so totally that they cannot see it any other way—and they won't change. What these men do is externalize their conflicts—this means that they find fault outside themselves. Phil's behavior, however, is more directly expressed—he doesn't blame Regina for his feelings—and his problem can be resolved.

A man can use his powerful primal feelings to make changes in his life. Art had wanted to break up with Emily for a long time, but each time he left her, he'd always come back. Soon he would feel engulfed again and, again, wrench himself away. He discussed this painful pattern with us, and finally began to prepare to leave, once and for all. But he wanted to act responsibly and be sure that both of them were prepared emotionally and financially for the break. Together, the couple set a date, and Art moved out.

After that, he went home to see his mother. When he returned from this visit, he told us that for the first time in his life he didn't feel as if his mother's expectations and demands had absolute power over him. Until now, he'd always tried to please her while feeling at the same time that he was forever giving in to her. The only time he didn't feel engulfed was when he was hundreds of miles away.

With Emily, Art's feelings of closeness were matched by feelings of entrapment. As a child, he had never established firm ego boundaries that would allow him to have intimate relationships; the long shadow of childhood still hovered over him. We encouraged him *not* to get involved in another relationship until he had been comfortably on his own for a while. Once he'd established himself in his own home, he came to see that by breaking up with Emily, he had really been "breaking up" with his mother. Art is a Good Guy Today/Gone Tomorrow who may make a breakthrough, because even though he blows hot and cold about intimacy, most of his behavior is responsible. He talks about his feelings, so he may sound "weirder" than other men, but in reality, his feelings are normal and altogether typical.

Society tells men that in order to be male you have to walk away from your mother—at the age of three—and never look back. But during adolescence, separation and male identity come into the spotlight once again, and the personality is malleable. It almost seems as if the boy has a second chance to resolve the old issues. But for many men, society has the last word; by now, boys and girls have been ruthlessly segregated into two separate camps. At this point in the boy's life, his father may become very concerned with the boy's manliness (he sees the boy as a reflection of himself) and pushes the mother even further into the background. Identifying strongly with his father, the boy hones his resolve to be aggressive and controlling and, above all, *different from women.*

Fortunately, this is always a question of degree—not every young boy wants to be the most macho guy on the block. William, a Good Enough Guy discussed in chapter 1, told us about how in his late adolescence he experienced a reawakening of his old, close relationship with his mother. Even as he spoke about her, William's voice grew warm and humorous. His mother, he said, was on to the fact that he was smoking marijuana in his bedroom, and confronted him with it directly and nonjudgmentally. "I thought she was a very hip person," he says, "not a doting suburban mother. She didn't condone what I was doing, but she treated me like an adult who could make his own decisions." At this point the two became closer than they'd been for years—if not exactly confidantes, then interested and respectful of one another's values and insights and ideas. William has a basic love and respect for all the women in his life, a capacity not necessarily lacking in a good number of other men but more likely to be in a state of untapped potential.

We're impressed by several men we've known who had the ability as young adults to be close to their mothers. But a man must feel strong enough within himself that he can get close to and separate from his mother (and other women) at the same time. This is something like walking and bouncing a ball at the same time—it takes a certain amount of coordination. Getting close to a mother or another woman can always knock a man off balance. Women can ride the tightrope between separateness and connectedness because we never had to disconnect so wrenchingly from our mothers; we can be ourselves and love intimacy at the same time.

The Man of the Future

Nancy Chodorow and Dorothy Dinnerstein say that the best way to remedy men's problems with intimacy is to throw out the old, sex-defined parenting roles, open up the hallowed mother-child dyad and bring in Father. Harvard University psychoanalyst James Herzog writes about the psychological effect of physically absent fathers on young children. Herzog called the resulting phenomenon *father hunger.* Other researchers went a step further and wrote about the effects of the *psychologically* absent father, finding that the sons of these men are in deep trouble when it comes to intimate relationships. It is clear to us that if the primary caretakers are both Mother *and* Father, who are *equally* involved in the child's development, a boy would not have to reject intimacy in order to grow up male. He would have before him his father, a man who knows how to be intimate; finally, Mother could step down from the pedestal upon which she has been imprisoned by the worship—and dread—of her son.

We believe that it is up to today's generation of men to raise their sons differently. Many men who are conscious of their own early loss want to give their sons what they never had, but because these men have only taken baby steps in intimacy, their best intentions may collapse. Suddenly, a man balks at parenting—perhaps the most ongoing, rigorous form of intimacy of all—in the same way he's pulled up short in intimate relationships with women. But if men take this on, think of the brave new world before us! Boys will learn that it is normal—not dangerous—to be close to other people and sensitive to their needs. Boys will grow into men who will *not* assume that women live for them or that everything in a relationship must be on their terms. Nor will these men feel a need to dominate, control, or withdraw from women; closeness and equality with women will no longer mean that a guy must "surrender" to her. There *are* some small signs of society's change: fathers who take leaves of absence from work to care for children, which was unheard of five or ten years ago. Some corporations are moving in this direction as well, with policies that enable fathers to take time off after the birth or adoption of a child. This is the only the very beginning of a remarkable, evolutionary trend.

Men are slowly changing. But at this point in your life, you may feel frustrated and hopeless. As women grow stronger, more assertive, and self-confident, and as they expect something in return from men for the first time, men are more fearful than ever before. But this is the last generation of men for whom it was socially acceptable to be raised by Mother only, with Father barely visible in the deep background, and we'd like to think that it's the last generation who will have major commitment problems as a result of outdated parenting. *That* is reason for hope.

Women's problems with being comfortably autonomous have been talked to death. We're all sick of hearing how women are "good at" intimacy but have trouble being separate and independent. From the same family crucible, we came out with this deficit. But counting from when the contemporary feminist movement began, we're a good twenty years ahead of men in making up our deficit; up until now, men haven't even acknowledged theirs.

Now we will go one step further than the new theorists. Because women are intimacy experts, they have to help men make changes—which doesn't mean solving their problems for them! In the old days, a woman would do it all for a man—and do it so well he wouldn't even know she was doing it. We say that for him to change, he has to know the problem first. You are stuck—you can't do it for him, back away from the challenge, or foist him off on a shrink. It has to happen at home.

In the couples work we do, we see women and men who are out of synch. Women have caught up with men in what men do best—autonomy—but men are beginners at intimacy. Things are obviously off balance, and the source of the problem is just as obvious. It isn't so much a question of adjusting the imbalance as it is giving the man the time and skills he needs to catch up.

We're both teaching workshops on gender differences and intimacy—people know that the effects of these differences constitute the underlying theme of their daily lives. Thankfully, the clinical basis has already been laid. Now we're analyzing men and women and examining the implications of the research.

Jeff, a client of ours, came to a session one day and with a puzzled look on his face told us about a strange incident. He'd had sex with his girlfriend, Marcia, and afterward, for some reason he couldn't fathom, found himself crying. He had been embarrassed—he never cried—and he'd felt somehow weak, not in control as he usually was. But as we talked, he slowly came to understand what had happened to him. The intensity of fusion with Marcia had been overwhelming. "I've never been so close to another person," he'd told her, "and it frightens me. I think I'm getting to love you too much."

Jeff's tears aren't typical, but his emotions are. Many men wonder how intimacy can feel so good and so terrifying at the same time. Jeff struggles to answer the riddle: why a sense of danger should permeate his most intimate moments with the woman he loves. This is the question we think most men will be facing in their own lives soon.

In the next chapter, we'll talk about the defenses a man uses to avoid commitment.

6

Talk, Dark, and Distant: Men and Their Defenses

When Kevin, a 34-year-old importer/exporter with dark, curly hair, a quick smile, and a runner's wiry body, first walked into our office, we were impressed by his apparent self-assurance. His manner was smooth and confident, and he wore his Brooks Brothers three-piece suits with casual grace. Over the course of several interviews we watched as cracks in the façade began to emerge, as Kevin edged closer to understanding that something was very wrong with his life.

First there was Danielle. "She was the most exotic, gorgeous woman I'd ever seen," he told us. When he first spotted her seated near him in a bar, he impulsively wrote down his phone number on a matchbook and sent it over to her. Thrilled, he watched Danielle approach him. The two had a drink together and talked—Danielle, it turned out, was a French linguist vacationing in Manhattan—and Kevin was even more fascinated. She was so interesting, so full of ideas and opinions and a million impressions of city life. There was no question that the two would go to Kevin's apartment and to bed. And this, Kevin says, turned out to be the best night he'd ever spent with a woman. Danielle postponed her return flight to Europe for several weeks so that they could spend time together.

The next time the couple saw one another was in Paris, when Kevin was on a business trip. Oddly, while still infatuated, Kevin now felt insecure and inferior to Danielle, who was so accomplished in languages and art, and so flamboyant and unusual in her manner and style of dress. Without his being aware of it, a change was taking place in his feelings toward Danielle: at first he'd loved her sophistication, but now he secretly wished she were less accomplished, less beautiful—just *less*. She'd never tone herself down, he decided; she'd always be a little too wild and a little too interesting. Now he felt unbelievably insecure. He imagined her outwitting him in front of his friends or being outrageously smart and erudite about everything from politics to art. They'd been to some parties together, and she'd been dismayingly articulate and self-confident; beside her, he'd felt dull and uninteresting. He resented her for this, resented her for her ambition and eagerness to get ahead. She made him feel little and weak. She made him feel *put down.*

Meanwhile, over their next several visits, Danielle fell in love with Kevin. She told him she'd begun investigating the possibility of moving to New York. "We're not right for each other," he told her. "You're artsy. I'm conservative. We're too different."

Danielle understood a little about Kevin's insecurity, but not the full extent of it. She assured him that she admired and respected him, and that she enjoyed their differences. Couldn't he learn to enjoy them, too? After all, this was what had brought them together in the first place.

But Kevin said no. Even their sexual relationship was no good anymore; as he put it, "All the stars and moons have to be in the right place," or sex leaves him cold. As far as he was concerned, all that remained was to say good-bye. And suddenly, the most exciting relationship of his life was all over.

In the months that followed, Kevin discovered that Danielle had given his life color and drama and a special sort of piquancy;

without her, things washed out to monotonous gray. He thought he wanted color in his life—thought he wanted *her*—but he'd been wrong. He decided to put Danielle out of his mind. There were lots of other women; for example, Sandy, a new executive in his office, who had recently caught his eye. . . .

Listening to men talk about failed, drained, aborted, or ambivalent relationships, we were struck by a typical tone of bewilderment. These men sensed that their relationships weren't working and their lives weren't adding up, but they didn't know why. Sometimes, as a man spoke, his uneasiness would be thick enough to cut with a knife, although he would not be able to name the unease or its cause.

Uneasiness, discomfort, confusion—relationships create subterranean levels of anxiety that surface in these feelings men don't name. At the same time, men will use unconscious defenses to cope with conflict and anxiety. These are not isolated cases—we were able to identify an entire group of defenses men use to keep fear and anxiety at bay.

A defense works something like this: when a conflict leads to anxiety, a man's psyche mobilizes against it. Now he has a buffer—a defense—that either removes the anxiety or disguises it so that he is protected from its sting. We all know how bad anxiety feels—the sole purpose of a defense is to soothe it.

A "good" defense will help a person function well in his life and keep his relationships on an even keel; a "bad" defense will stand in the way of making good relationships. For many men, their defenses make successful relationships with women almost impossible to achieve.

In our culture, all of us learn defenses as a response to anxiety, but boys learn the lesson all too well. Anna Freud talks about how little boys, three years old and in the midst of the Oedipal conflict, pretend to be supermen in response to feelings of vulnerability and helplessness. By identifying with a powerful figure, a child denies the reality that he is little and weak. Boys also learn to *externalize* their problems—put the blame for difficulties "out there"—as a way to distance themselves in relation-ships. This is the basis for the distancing mechanisms men use later in life.

In our offices, what we're seeing among some men is an exaggeration—or a hardening—of that early childhood defen-siveness. Now that men feel more threatened by women, the general anxiety level has shot up, which means that more ex-treme forms of primitive defenses are being mustered to control women and to create distance from them. But being critical of this hard-line defensive posture is taken as an attack on men; "This is just the way men *are*," we're told. At the same time we hear, "Women have defenses, too!"

Of course they do. But we want to describe the defenses men are using today in response to their new anxiety about women. Here are six of the most common types. Some are unhealthier than others and are more likely to be used by Good For Nothing Guys; others are more penetrable. A man may use *any or all of them* at one time or another.

It is not your responsibility to change a man's defenses—our advice is to be aware of his defenses and to assess the degree to which he defends himself in dealing with you. Using this as-sessment will help you place him in one of the three categories of men, and then you will know what to expect from him in terms of capability for commitment.

1. Splitting. A child sees his mother either as "all good" or "all bad"—when she is "good" he can't remember her when she was "bad," and vice versa. Eventually, the child puts the two sides together and understands that Mother can be both gratifying and depriving.

It is very common these days to find a man compartmentaliz-ing a woman's traits into those that are "good" and others that are "bad." Until recently, women suppressed parts of themselves, which made things much easier for men. As long as women were meek and quiet, relationships were not so complex, but now that women are far more complete in themselves, men have found new sets of demands placed on them.

What does this defense do for a man? It allows him to keep a woman in a holding pattern while he analyzes her behavior. He may actually make up a list, adding up her debits and credits, constantly weighing the balance; she's too-this and not-enough-that. To give himself the sense that he's in control, a man may try to pick a complex woman apart.

Sam has been involved with Gina for two years. "I can talk to her about personal things," he says. "I've never talked to any other woman the way I can talk to her. When I'm high-strung, she unstrings me." At the same time, when Gina doesn't make brilliant cocktail party conversation (she's shy), he becomes critical. "Does she stimulate me intellectually?" he asks himself and tells himself she doesn't; in fact, she's "a bore." At this point Sam completely forgets the side of Gina that's loving, nurturing, and generous (the "good" side) and completely forgets what an important part of his life she is. For Sam, when Gina is good, she is very, very good; and when she is bad, she is horrid. He changes his mind from one minute to the next; he is on an emotional seesaw. Sam can't see that Gina—and any other woman he might ever become involved with, for that matter—is made up of many different qualities, some of which are okay with him and others not so okay. So, when he is dissatisfied with Gina, he temporarily blanks out everything he likes about her and has affairs with other women.

For Gina, the situation is tortuous. She is made to feel inadequate, as if she simply can't be what he wants her to be. One minute, she is "in," the next minute she is "out." He flattens her into a one-dimensional stick figure by reducing her to lists of qualities—acceptable and unacceptable. As long as he can paint her in broad strokes without the nuances and shadings of character, she is less of a threat.

Sam, with his harsh criticisms and affairs, is a Good For Nothing Guy. There are many other men who will "split" women without being as stuck as he is. However, even a Good Enough Guy may call upon this defense to deal with a situation that seems menacing to him.

2. Projective Identification.

2. *Projective Identification.* This defense is the core of all couple relationships. One of the reasons you are attracted to your partner is that this person has qualities you haven't been able to develop in yourself. For example, the man may be extravagant with money, while the woman is cautious. Part of his attraction to her is that he is uncomfortable denying himself anything; part of her attraction to him is that she is uncomfortable giving herself anything. If the relationship works well, he learns to be more careful, and she learns to be more generous.

But what we find today is that often a man will be repelled by the very characteristics in a woman that initially attracted him. Kevin, at the beginning of this chapter, ended three relationships before he began to understand that the reason for his simultaneous attraction and revulsion toward a woman is that she embodied qualities that he had expelled from himself.

Kevin disowned flamboyance and vibrancy in his personality and unconsciously chose women who would fill in the holes. Unfortunately, his "other half" turned out to be too threatening.

Paul is similar to Kevin, but not as extreme. He and Cynthia are both trial lawyers. Cynthia has a colorful style that serves her well in the courtroom, and most of the time Paul thinks, "What an exciting woman!" But sometimes her penchant for exaggeration rubs him the wrong way.

Paul is sedate and rather stuffy; Cynthia is loose and flamboyant. His attraction to her is powerful, but he wishes she'd button up once in a while. Meanwhile, even though Cynthia knows very well that Paul doesn't like her to exaggerate her stories, she keeps doing it because she *likes* telling stories her way. This couple is in a bind—what originally attracted Paul now threatens him.

Historically, a woman has been the person-who-completes-the-man. In the traditional marriage, two people added up to one; the woman's contribution was undervalued as the "finishing touches" applied to a man's personality. Now women are more likely to develop into complex people on their own and less likely to flow into the empty spaces in a man's personality—*and* less likely to change something they like about themselves if it threatens a man. Paul eventually realized that "Cynthia's problem" was really *his* problem, and that it wasn't up to her to change. It was up to him to come to terms with his attraction to a complex woman.

3. Idealization/The Perfect Woman.   A great number of men we talked to shared with us their endless search for the Perfect Woman. She isn't the same for every man, and she seems strangely indefinable when you get right down to it—but still the search goes on.

The Perfect Woman is a defense, too. While the Omni-Available Woman is more than just a defense (in reality, there *are* more available single women than there are men), the Perfect Woman is a total figment of a man's imagination; she goes back to the time when his mother existed for him alone, with no other function or purpose in life.

Imagining his Perfect Woman, David sat back in his chair and gazed out the window. No, he couldn't exactly tell us what she looked like, nor could he say what she was like as a person. How will he know her when he sees her? What a mundane question! He will just know, that's all, that she is "the one." The pattern many men follow when they meet a real woman goes like this: fall fast, make her into the Perfect Woman, find her first flaw, decide she isn't "it." What a set-up!

When we describe the Perfect Woman fantasy/defense to friends and colleagues, they often counter with, "Women want perfect partners, too; everyone wants a perfect partner—show me the person who doesn't!"

We agree. Any woman who has what we call a savior fantasy is not alone; it is the most common women's fantasy. Women who were raised to be top-notch students and career women also learned early on that someday their prince would come along and "save" them from having to take care of themselves. Women were dilettantes in independence then—a man was a woman's real career. "That's the way I think, and so do all my friends," said one woman honestly. "I'm trying to get established at work, and I've spent lots of money decorating my studio apartment, but I still think about that guy on the white charger who'll sweep me up and take me away." She laughed. "But it's ridiculous," she added, "we all know that." It's true—we don't know any woman who honestly believes in this guy. "It's my fantasy," another woman told us. "He—with a capital H, of course!—will ring my buzzer downstairs, get past the doorman, and knock on my door. 'Hi!' he'll say, 'I'm a little late, but I showed up, didn't I?' "

But haven't we all heard enough about women's savior fantasies? At least women can be ironic about them! Newer and more relevant is the unveiling of the Perfect Woman. In our culture, she has been protected and safeguarded, and men have never had to gaze into the fantasy's face and watch it crumble. They have never had to laugh at themselves and say, "I keep trying to find the Perfect Woman, even though I know she doesn't exist. Isn't it idiotic?"

At this point many men really do expect the Perfect Woman to ring the buzzer in the lobby, knock on the door, and say, "Here I am." She is the woman who will be there all the time for a man and meet all his needs. As long as he is expecting her at any moment, he doesn't have to deal with a real woman. With today's real woman, he may be frustrated or even rejected. Most striking of all about this fantasy is that most men feel absolutely *entitled* to have a Perfect Woman. At one time his mother revolved around him like the earth around the sun and satisfied all his desires. Now men see women as potential re-creators of these wonderful narcissistic moments when nothing in the universe existed beyond himself and she-who-fulfilled-his-every-desire. Heavenly, but we're supposed to grow up and come down to earth.

The Perfect Woman may suddenly show up when you least expect her. On the first anniversary of his relationship with Corinne, Douglas suggested that they plan a vacation together in Europe. He also surprised her one day when she'd been talking about reupholstering her furniture by saying, "Wait, don't do it all. Let's decide what *we* will need." Corinne was pleased and at the same time a little nervous; their relationship had been building slowly over this year, and "slow" suited her just fine. At 29, she wasn't in a hurry to get married; she'd simply been enjoying the way her relationship with Douglas had been deepening. Only recently, their sex life had become more satisfying; she'd always been uninhibited, and now Douglas had opened up. She felt lucky to have Douglas; he wanted to spend time with her, he wanted them to be monogamous, and he wasn't trying to push her into anything she wasn't ready for.

Then one Friday night, soon after they began discussing vacation plans, she had the feeling that something was wrong. He was restless and uncommunicative, and he was smoking again (he'd quit recently). "What's wrong?" she asked him at last.

"I really feel that I need some space," he told her after a long moment of silence. "I like you, but it isn't the same as it was. If it were really right between you and me, I wouldn't have these doubts. I—I just don't know if you're the one."

Corinne was horrified. She remembered all the times he'd told her he loved her. She told Douglas, "Don't worry, I want our relationship to develop just as it has been. I don't want to get married now. I'm not pushing this. I almost feel as if *you* have been pushing *me!*"

"I just can't see you for a while," Douglas said.

Since he was experiencing doubts and anxiety, Douglas decided that Corinne was the source. If she were exactly what he wanted (although he was foggy about what that was), then he would not be doubtful. Unfortunately, many men want and expect women to make life smooth and easy for them—there should be no imperfections, he should feel no anxiety. If he does feel anxious, a man will not automatically look to himself for the cause. (This is the reason why in psychological testing men so often come out looking "healthier" than women do.) A man is not likely to say, "I'm anxious"; he is likely to say, *"She* is my problem." To Douglas, Corinne was the problem—not his own conflicts about commitment.

4. The Counter-Phobic Response. The more involved Douglas became, the more he was afraid. To combat the fear, he whipped up his own enthusiasm for the relationship and pushed it up a level (*he* suggested the vacation, *he* hinted at living together). Douglas needed to master his fear, but only succeeded in masking it, so that eventually it exploded. He'd gone *too* far, *too* fast—and then he had to get out fast.

Corinne was placed in one of the worst positions a woman can be in. Douglas didn't exactly say the failure of the relationship had been her fault, but he did say that if he'd been more in love with her, this terrible thing wouldn't have happened. She felt as if her self-esteem had been run over by a truck.

All the same, she told Douglas that he was fearful of commitment, and that he should go into therapy. In our session with her, she was not quite so composed. She asked us if there weren't something she could do to "make things better."

"No," we said. "This is a terrible situation for you, but this is precisely the point when you can't do a thing. Don't call him—this is his time for soul searching. The ball's in his court."

"But he's too good to lose," Corinne said. "I'll wait for him." We knew how she felt. When you've put in a year of your life, learned the quirks and hidden parts of another personality, set up certain routines with one another, and experienced a gradually deepening closeness and trust, giving it all up practically overnight is devastating.

Either Douglas will realize that he's given up the best thing in his life, or he won't. If Corinne decides to "wait," what exactly is she supposed to do? Take up knitting, or perhaps folk dancing? The answer is clear. She *can't* wait—she has to get on with her life. We interviewed one woman whose relationship "ended" for this same reason; then the couple saw one another off and on for the next three years. Finally, they got married—but in general, you can't count on this. Maybe when you're 25, "waiting and seeing" is okay, but when you're nearly 30, you haven't got the time.

"I feel so terrible," Corinne told us. "What do you think about my seeing someone new this weekend? There's this guy I know . . ."

"Great," we said. "Have a terrific time."

5. *Disillusionment/The Bitch.* The flip side of the Perfect
Woman, the Bitch is a man's nightmare—the wicked witch and
the ugly stepmother who eat men alive for breakfast. Even
though he may actually be attracted to an aggressive, self-confident woman, he is at the same time, deep in his guts, repelled by
her. The Bitch is a throwback to when a man perceived his
mother as punitive, controlling, or demanding. Then she had
power over him, and he was little and weak. For all he knew, she
really could swallow him up.

Jana told us a story: she and her boyfriend, Dave, were
taking a tour of the California wine country. Their guide was a
striking, self-confident woman in her twenties who knew her
subject inside and out. "She's terrific," Jana whispered to Dave.
At which point he leaned over to her and said, "Are you kidding?
She's a bitch."

"I was *horrified,*" Jana told us. "I mean, I thought I knew this
guy. I asked him later what had bothered him so much about the
tour guide. At first he couldn't say, but then he said that she acted
as if she were casting pearls before swine. He said that she'd just
strutted around, assuming everyone was fascinated by every
word."

Jana pointed out to Dave that this woman didn't have to
check out what she was saying with her audience; since she knew
her stuff, she didn't need anyone else's stamp of approval. Reluctantly, Dave agreed. But Jana could tell that his gut response
really hadn't changed.

In the dictionary, a bitch is, in addition to being a female dog,
a "lewd, immoral, or domineering woman." In more modern
terms, she is a castrator, a ballbreaker. In reality, a woman who
is called a bitch may be goal-oriented, sure of herself, and un-
apologetic about who she is and what she wants. She is not
accommodating to other people's desires; nor does she exist to
please other people.

Many men have learned that women are supposed to
change their opinions, demeanors, and minds in order to suit a
man. If a woman truly doesn't care, this may be galling.

In our society, when a man is threatened by a woman, he

may say she's a bitch. The fact is, he's afraid of her. At a party, one man couldn't take his eyes off a stunning, self-confident woman. He fantasized that he would approach her, but didn't. He worked himself up into a sweat of fear and anticipation, making countless false moves in her direction. "I'm a good-looking guy," he told himself. "She'd be lucky to go home with me." But deep in his insecure soul, this man couldn't imagine that such a desirable woman would ever want him. Rather than admit his fear, he finally shrugged his shoulders and thought, "She's got to be a bitch. I know it just by looking at her," and left without speaking to her.

A man may also fear that a woman will be ballsy enough to be just as self-involved as he is. He knows *he* doesn't want to be docile, sweet, or nice; he knows *he* is out for himself—what will it mean if she is, too? Two Wall Street investment bankers in their early thirties discussed why "Wall Street women" may be business buddies but never marriage partners. These women are the ultimate bitches—aggressive, out for themselves, women with a real "killer instinct." As they speak, the men's voices echo the disgust they feel for these women; if a woman isn't the soft, white underbelly of a man, she is, to some men, loathsome.

But a woman doesn't have to have the "killer instinct" in order to be called a bitch. All she really has to be is strong, assertive, and purposeful; men are so threatened by these traits in a woman that the term bitch is often hurled as a man's ultimate trump card. "I see why I'm unhappy with you—you're a bitch!"

6. *Intimidation and Bullying.* (Like the Bitch, this is not a clinical term, but a term used to describe male defensive behavior.) On their first night at Club Med, four Manhattan working women on vacation together sat with a group of men at dinner. Dana offered to go to the dessert table and bring back desserts for everyone. When she returned to the table, one man looked at the tray with disgust and said he didn't like anything she'd chosen. Dana realized with a shock that he meant her to go back and get something else for him! Instead of doing so, she returned to her seat. "When I get married," joked this man, a dentist in his late twenties, to the table at large, "the first thing I'm going to do is send my wife to maid school."

Dana wasn't laughing. She realized that by not obediently returning to the dessert table, she'd provoked fear and rage in the seemingly unassuming dentist. In this case, a man may react by trying to put you down or taking a drill to your dignity. His message to you is "You think you're so smart; well, you'd better be nicer to men or you'll never get married." Don't be surprised when a man reacts with verbal attacks to what he perceives as your "aggressiveness" or "uppitiness."

In 1985, a Roper poll showed that 43 percent of men surveyed preferred women who would fulfill traditional roles in marriage, such as taking care of the home. Why do so many men want their wives to get a college degree and then stay home and push a mop? For some Good For Nothing Guys, just the fact that you exist as an independent, intelligent individual is a capital offense, and they'd like nothing better than to see you barefoot and pregnant forever. For most men, the threat is not so cosmic that it can't be wrestled down to earth. But if you find yourself in Dana's situation, take your beach blanket to the far end of the pool and work on your tan until something better comes along.

What goes into the making of a bully? Let's say a small boy has an aggressive father. Huge and terrifying, the father looms over him; the child quakes in his shoes and "resolves" the fear by modeling himself after the big bully lording it over him. When the boy feels threatened by anyone—his mother, for example— he unconsciously acts toward her just as his father does: by trying to control or dominate her. By the time he's an adult, he feels justified in insulting and outraging any woman who crosses his path.

Three Men and Their Defenses

Most men use one more of the defenses we've described. The extent to which a man uses them can help you pinpoint your guy's position on the commitment-fearing spectrum.

"Christine used to be fun," said Phillip. "Now she's pushing too hard. I told her I was a loner, and I liked it that way. But women never listen. They think it's a challenge! But I never misrepresent myself with a woman—on the first date I'll tell her, don't try to nail me."

Phillip, who is in his forties, has never been married, and is an example of a Good For Nothing Guy who is defended to the nth degree. "My mother was an angry bitch," he told us, "so I figured it was better not to marry. And it's great—I never have to ask anybody, where do you want to eat, what do you want to eat, what time do you want to eat? Marriage is no good for me because I don't like to compromise."

Phillip's father "acted single" by spending as little time as possible with his family; when he was around, he and Phillip's mother fought, finally splitting up when Phillip was in college. Phillip has lots of women friends and all the sex he wants. Women in their twenties are his favorites because "they aren't interested in marriage yet"; by the time they're in their thirties, they want a relationship and "that's a drag."

"I never seduce women," Phillip said. "I wait for them to seduce me." He then went on to explain with complete aplomb that if a woman is too sexually aggressive, he "can't get it up. She has to be just aggressive enough." Phillip has to *allow* a woman to seduce him; she can't do it on her terms. If she keeps trying it her way, "I stop seeing her; it obviously isn't right."

Phillip has absolutely no intimate relationships. "What if you need a shoulder to cry on?" we asked him.

"I never do," he replied serenely. "I convinced myself nothing would ever bother me, and nothing ever does." All of Phillip's feelings are smoothed over and blunted, as if with sandpaper; he has no passions, no attachments, no needs, no desires.

To attain this state of male nirvana, Phillip has become a master of defense—he will never see a woman as a composite; she will be forever split. Women who are "aggressive" are quickly labeled "bitches." If the Perfect Woman existed, he'd find something wrong with her. There *is* no woman for Phillip—not even in his imagination. The most fascinating thing about him, though, is that as indefensibly Good For Nothing as Phillip is, he is a nice guy in all areas except relationships. He is popular with friends and colleagues, and he always brings other people's children gifts when he comes to family holidays. But a woman should not be fooled by this guy—he says who he is and he means it.

Other men admire him from afar—he's almost a male ideal. "Hey, the guy has a great life," said one happily married man we know. "He's free. You're judging him by female standards."

But the fact is that from a mental health point of view, intimacy is defined as *a necessary part* of adulthood. In our culture, the male deficiency in intimacy has been ignored. But with women no longer willing to pick up the slack in relationships, what was merely obvious before has become glaringly unavoidable.

For the Good Enough Guy, defenses are like handy gadgets he picks up when he needs them—they aren't built into his character. Fred is perfectly aware that Elaine is more professionally successful than he is and makes a far better salary. He also loves the fact that she is so successful, but in a few subtle ways he denies to himself that she's quite as much of a star as she really is. Elaine pays all the expenses; by the end of the month, she's broke. Fred, on the other hand, contributes nothing except for vacations and investments; he controls all the discretionary income. "I'm the man of the house," Fred told us. "I'm in charge." And we could see that this was a denial mechanism that worked for him—and for the couple. It doesn't bother Elaine when he says this; she knows it isn't true, but instinctively, she also knows that being the boss is important to him. Her pretense is her gift to him.

For Fred, thinking he's the boss is the fulfillment of a wish. Sometimes, he wishes Elaine were an old-fashioned, compliant woman, but this is a fairly muted fantasy. A Good Enough Guy doesn't think in terms of the Bitch or the Perfect Woman because, for him, women are real people made up of many traits. He doesn't have to split a woman because he is basically more comfortable with a multi-dimensional woman than he is with a cartoon. (Again, we can probably trace this relative defenselessness in the Good Enough Guy to his relationship with his mother, in which he most likely maintained a closeness, while keeping his own boundaries intact.)

You need to pay attention to the kind of defenses a man uses and how often he uses them. He may say things such as Jack said to Nina in chapter 3: "I hate it when you're angry with me; I like you when you're sweet." This is an obvious form of splitting—he wants her *only* to be nice. Or sometimes he'll criticize you for the very things you *know* are attractive to him—let's say that one day, he likes you because you're emotional and vibrant, while the next day he seems disgruntled because you talk too much. Or he may like the fact that you're sexy, and then get on your case for being flirtatious. In mild forms, these defenses are not harmful to your self-esteem or to the relationship.

For the Good Guy Today/Gone Tomorrow, defenses are less a part of his character than they are for the Good For Nothing Guy. The Good Guy Today finds his defenses somewhat alien and uncomfortable. Part of him wishes he could shrug them off. On the other hand, his defenses can seriously block, bewilder—and even torture—him in his attempts at intimacy.

After Kevin broke up with Danielle, the French linguist, he met Sophia, an advertising executive. They dated for a while, until Kevin decided that even though she was outgoing and gregarious, which he liked, she was really a bit of a "loudmouth." Worse, she wasn't "intellectual" enough for his tastes. Worse yet, even though sex had been great at the beginning, once he got involved, "the sex was off." If things weren't "perfect" between himself and a woman, Kevin would feel an emptiness, a dulling of his senses, where there'd once been desire. It was a flat, gray feeling, like the depression he'd felt after he and Danielle split up.

When he told Sophia his misgivings about her, she signed off, leaving Kevin to brood on his fate. Why did he have such bad luck with women? Why couldn't he find the right one? On the other hand, what if his fault-finding in women was a sign of a problem in himself? Maybe he criticized women so that he didn't have to face his own weaknesses. But Kevin immediately pushed these disturbing thoughts out of his head—he decided to forget about Sophia and Danielle and find that perfect woman he knew was out there somewhere.

Then he met Melanie, a personnel director. "She was perfect in every way," he said. She was dynamic, ambitious, bursting with energy for work and relationships. When he was with her, Kevin felt as if he were in a state of perpetual sexual arousal. However, it wasn't long before he felt some familiar twinges—Did this woman actually have more on the ball than he did? And wasn't she a little too hard-edged in her approach to her career? Sometimes, he'd watch her at a party—she looked too damn good. And why didn't she pay more attention to him at parties? He could never marry a woman who acted as if he weren't even alive.

Meanwhile, as a few months passed, Melanie became more involved with Kevin and began to take more interest in spending time alone with him. If they did go to parties, she stayed by his side; she talked to him less about her work and more about her strong feelings for him.

Kevin was squirming. Now that Melanie was actively trying to please him, he couldn't stand it. Finally, he came up with a "laundry list" of her faults: sitting at his kitchen table one night with paper and pencil, he scribbled them all out: first, that she was "too deferring"; second, that she "didn't fight enough"; and finally, that she was "too available—she should see other men."

Melanie took one look at Kevin's "laundry list" and threw it in his face, calling him selfish and inconsistent, as well as an emotional ice-cube. First, he'd criticized her for not paying enough attention to him, and then, when she did focus on him, all he could do was bemoan the fact that she was no longer feisty!

"If only she'd done what I wanted, then everything would have been perfect," Kevin told himself mournfully. Well, Melanie just hadn't been the right one. But around now, something in Kevin started changing, and this was when he first came to see us. "I keep finding fault with women," he told us, "but I really want to have a relationship."

We explained the concept of splitting to Kevin, as well as

some of the other defenses he uses, and told him this was his way of making women less of a threat to him.

He smiled ironically. "I'm in a mess, aren't I?" he said.

Then he told us how he'd called Melanie the other night, to see if they might see one another once in a while. She'd hung up on him. "You know," Kevin told us near the end of the session, "I'll probably get married one of these days soon, and it probably won't be to anyone as great as she is."

Soon after this, when he was invited to his friend Joshua's wedding, he felt envious, and when he was there he thought about Melanie. He'd wanted her to be who *he* wanted her to be—not the person she really was. He'd expected her to suit all his moods and fulfill his crazy quilt of expectations. The wedding was the blackest day of Kevin's life.

In the next year, more of his friends got married. He joked that at the age of 35, he was beginning to feel like everyone's favorite bachelor uncle. To cheer himself up, he called in a decorator to redo his apartment. "Make it exciting and unusual," he instructed the decorator; and was left with black walls, minimalist furniture unfit for the human anatomy, and three gigantic, hostile-looking cactus plants.

Sitting in his chic, unlivable apartment, all Kevin could think about was eating Chinese food in bed with Melanie and going out for the Sunday newspapers and hot croissants. Sometimes he still blamed her for the breakup of their relationship; other times, he sat still with the chilly knowledge that he'd broken it into a million irreparable pieces himself.

But Kevin is more aware, more insightful. He sees and accepts different aspects of himself—the first step toward accepting the many aspects of a woman. Intimacy is made of two complex people, whose personalities are filled with subtleties and nuances, each of whom is aware of the other's depths and shadings. What will happen to Kevin? He could become a fully realized man instead of a too-well-defended man.

We've shown you who today's man is, why he doesn't commit and where his problems come from. With this knowledge, and using the Five Levels of Commitment, you should be able to analyze your relationship and find the degree of intimacy you're at now. In the next section, we'll show you some practical strategies for dealing with men who have cold feet, including ways to get a man to give emotionally; what to do when you're ready to have a child and he's not; how to deal with marriage to an uncommitted man; and more. We've also included a special chapter for you to tear out and give to your guy to read—"For Men Only"—that will help him see his commitment problems and begin to take responsibility for his actions.

If the guy you're involved with begins doing any of the following, he's using typical male defenses to avoid his problems with intimacy:

- He makes "laundry lists" of your good and bad qualities, splitting you into a "good" or "bad" girlfriend without realizing that you are a composite of many qualities.
- He begins to criticize the very qualities in you that initially attracted him. For instance, initially he loved the fact that you were outgoing and lively at parties; now when you get home from a party he complains that you attracted too much attention to yourself or "made a fool of yourself".
- He's looking for the perfect woman; just when you feel that you're getting along well, he lets on that there's probably "someone better" out there for him, if only he could find her.
- He feels that successful, self-assured women are "bitches."
- He gets his own way by bullying you, often in front of others.

Part Two

BREAKING THE COMMITMENT BARRIER

7

Relationship Strategies

Even if your relationship is in danger of going under, you don't have to give up on it. There are specific ways to approach relationship problems—practices mainly used in couples therapy—that you can do on your own to overcome commitment stalemates. The cardinal rule to remember is that *all* men are conflicted about intimacy. Once you realize that, you're way ahead of the game. Then you can use the levels of commitment to evaluate him, yourself, and the relationship. From our work with couples, we've devised a seven-point, hands-on program for men with cold feet. These strategies can be used with Levels Two through Five; just make sure you're at least past casual dating before using them. It's easy—follow this program, and you will be on your way to a more committed relationship.

Program for the Commitment-Fearing Man (and You)

All of the following examples specifically address men's problems with intimacy, but require a woman's full participation. You will need to tell your partner that you feel the relationship is going nowhere, and that you want to improve your communication skills. It's all you need to say right now. Tell him to enter into these exercises with a sense of fun. If he refuses to participate at all, he will probably never be able to commit anyway—and the earlier you realize this and start looking for a Good Enough Guy, the better!

Exercise 1. Do Something Nice for Each Other Once a Day. (Simple, you say? Deceptively.) Don't tell your partner what the "nice thing" is you're doing for him; just do it, and write it down on a piece of paper. Have him do the same for you. *Do not discuss this with him.* Meanwhile, each of you must try to guess what nice thing the other has done and write *that* down. At the end of the week, each of you should have a list of seven things you've done for your partner and seven things he or she has done for you.

Often, people misunderstand what we mean when we say "Do something nice." It doesn't mean going out and buying him an expensive watch, and it definitely doesn't mean buying a woman a sexy negligee. When one man did this, he was shocked to find that his partner didn't count it on her list as something nice he'd done for her! Why? Because he'd bought the negligee for *himself*—for *his* pleasure, not hers.

This exercise requires: 1. recognizing that your partner is separate and different from yourself; 2. recognizing that what makes *you* happy doesn't necessarily make him/her happy; and 3. being sensitive to and acknowledging your partner's small, loving gestures (which are the true nitty gritty of any relationship).

It's an excellent sign if a man likes this exercise, and, in fact, a lot of men we work with love it. Since it is difficult for men to give ("What will I have left for me if I give to her?"), the exercise makes giving more manageable for a man. While he is used to feeling that what she wants is global (everything), he now sees that he can give small, specific things to her without giving up himself.

This exercise helps couples become more sensitive to what they do for each other and whether they are doing the right things. If you find at the end of the week that your lists don't match (you didn't pick up on his nice things, and he didn't pick up on yours), treat this as a way to learn about each other. (In other words, don't fight about it—try it again next week.)

A good relationship is all about knowing *how to give and to get.* It's about keeping one another in mind, doing things for one another—not necessarily laying down your life for your partner, but doing "small" things. For one woman, it was the times that her lover waited up for her when she came back late from business trips. For another, it was a "treat" or flowers that he picked up for her on his way over to her apartment. For one man, it was a neck rub when he felt particularly stressed.

In a way, it *is* very simple—it's the small, thoughtful things that make you feel loved.

Exercise 2. Be Selfish—Once a Day.   This is the flip side of Exercise 1. Selfishness in small doses can reassure a man that even though he is in a relationship, he hasn't been "cornered." This exercise is good for women in that it forces them to be selfish once a day, something most women have trouble doing—there are no points for self-sacrifice. The only restriction in this exercise is that you can't *spring* your selfish act on your partner—you have to discuss it in advance. (You might call your partner during the day, for example, and tell him you've decided to play tennis with a friend after work, thereby missing dinner together. Or, if a woman wants to talk, a man can exercise the selfish option and say he'd rather take a nap—it's up to him.)

We routinely tell men that personal space is a right, and that being in a relationship should *not* mean being joined at the hip. Typically, a man will assume that once he's in a relationship, a woman will put the squeeze on his space until he's gasping for breath. Exercise 2 shows couples that space is as organic and necessary to a relationship as is intimacy. Too much intimacy *is* stifling—do *you* want someone breathing down your neck twenty-four hours a day?

Exercise 3. More Selfishness.   Stuart and Phyllis are on a swing shift: either they are immersed in their work and don't see each other for days at a time, or else they spend huge, intense amounts of time together. When they're together, they're so involved sexually and emotionally that they often don't know when they've had enough. Then they start to fight about everything, including the way they sleep together. If they were really in love, they reason, they'd sleep wrapped in each other's arms; in fact, they spend most nights fighting over the covers. One of our first suggestions was that they buy a king-size bed. "You two need plenty of space," we told them. "You need to be able to stretch out."

We meant that not only literally, but figuratively. Everyone in a relationship needs to stretch. One time, after they hadn't seen each other for a week, Stuart and Phyllis spent several days and nights together. On their fourth morning, they were lying in bed in Stuart's apartment, talking and laughing, when out of the blue, Phyllis said, "Stuart, you're such a slob I can hardly stand being in your apartment." Stuart withdrew from her as if he'd been stung.

Any couple has to know that *there's a limit to how close they want to be.* It's *okay* to breathe, especially after you've been very intimate. Unknowingly, Phyllis was reacting to their days of closeness—and if she hadn't done it first, Stuart would have done something soon. Unfortunately, she wasn't aware that she needed breathing room; she didn't feel that it was "right" to need it. Instead, she picked a fight, since that's one guaranteed way to get immediate space!

To try to establish a balance between autonomy and closeness and to avoid the sort of nasty situation Phyllis and Stuart got into, we suggest that you:

1. Learn to identify the critical moment when you've had enough closeness.
2. Know that's it's *okay* to pull back when you need to.
3. Develop nonhurtful, nondestructive ways to ease away.

After a while, you will settle into a comfort level with your partner, in which it is fine simply to say something like, "I think I'll get up and take a shower now," or, "I think i'll go over to my apartment for a while." A need for privacy on the part of either one of you does *not* have to mean rejecting your partner.

Exercise 4. The Talking Cure.   You'll love this; he'll be skeptical. Each member of the couple takes fifteen-minute turns talking and listening to the other. Can a man slip around the Talking Cure by discussing last night's Mets game, the stock market, or the great new pasta recipe he saw in today's newspaper? No. *He must talk about his feelings.* While he does, you must listen without interrupting, grimacing, sighing, going to the bathroom, or making an "urgent" phone call. (In other words, you may not like what he says, but you still have to listen.) When he's through, you must repeat back to him what he said. Then he listens to you— without comment—and repeats back to you what *you* said.

Everyone knows men hate to talk about their feelings; with this exercise, he will be in serious training. Let's say he's angry at you for something you've done—last night you were tense at a dinner party; you snapped at him, and he was humiliated. Now he'll have to talk to you about it instead of withdrawing. The rule for you both is, "Do not accuse." This exercise is about *how you both feel about what is going on between you.*

This exercise is also excellent for teaching men the fine (and, unfortunately, mostly feminine) art of listening. You may find at first *no similarity* between what you said and what he *thinks* you said. Don't despair—as an exercise in tuning in to another person's feelings, this is similar to Exercise 1 and may take a good number of preliminary dry runs. However, do keep it to fifteen minutes. He may need more time to articulate, but after a while he may learn from you how to cover more ground.

Related to the Talking Cure is role-playing. Here, you switch roles—you play "him" and he plays "you"—and *listen*. When you play "him," imagine what it feels like to experience the squeeze of not enough space; when he plays "you," he may discover the part of him that needs more closeness. You don't have to master the Stanislavski acting method to do this exercise—the point is simply to *empathize* with one another's feelings.

For men who have trouble with role-playing, we put it like this: Become a lawyer for the opposition. Take her case and *win* it. (If he sees it as "a job," he'll jump in with both feet.) The point is that he has to empathize with you in order to argue your case effectively.

Lillian, 32, and Michael, 35, had been on Level Five, living together, for three years. Before that they'd dated monogamously for two years. Lillian wanted to begin discussing having children—and, naturally, getting married. She couldn't understand Michael's hesitation; he said he truly loved her (and acted like he did), and he seemed to be committed to her, too. Then why the hesitation over what should logically be the next step?

Lillian decided to try the Talking Cure. She set up a time each week when she and Michael would take each other's point of view and express it to the other. The first week Michael only tried half-heartedly; then, when it was Lillian's turn, she gave a very forceful presentation of what she thought were Michael's reasons for not wanting to get married. "Why rock the boat?" she said, as Michael. "Things are going so well now. I've got all the comforts of a marriage without the commitment. I want children but I'm in no rush; I can have kids five years from now, so why do it before I'm ready?"

By this time, Michael was sitting forward in his chair, listening intently.

"And furthermore," Lillian continued, now really getting into her role, "my parents didn't have such a hot marriage. My father wasn't ever there for my mom. Then, after she had slaved and cooked and cleaned for him for thirty years, Dad left her for his ten-years-younger secretary. I'm *terrified* that I may do the same thing to any woman if I ever got married."

Lillian stopped, amazed at what had come out of her mouth. Michael was staring at her wide-eyed. Suddenly he embraced her and started crying. After hours of talking, Michael came to realize that his fears actually stemmed from his father's desertion of his mother; he was afraid that if he married Lillian he'd wind up doing the same thing to her that his father had done to his mother. Once he'd brought these fears out into the open and was able to discuss them, he began to see how irrational they were. He *wasn't* his father, and Lillian was not his mother. Their marriage would have as good or as bad a chance as any other marriage would; in fact, Michael admitted, they'd have an even better chance because he felt they had a stronger relationship than most couples he knew.

Michael and Lillian had an unusually fast breakthrough— within a month they planned a small wedding, and, two years later, they are still married and Lillian is expecting their first child. The Talking Cure is valuable because it can bring out for discussion the problems a man has in commitment *in a totally non-threatening, objectified way.*

Exercise 5. Play Together/Stay Together. One couple, stalled out and sick of each other, sat in silent frustration in our office one day. As they talked, it turned out that in the past Sharon and Mark had played tennis, hiked, and gone to the beach together. But as they'd gotten closer, they'd given up their playtime for talking and hashing over problems until they were both numb. We told them their relationship was sinking from too much seriousness. They'd always loved playing together, so our recommendation was: talk less and play more!

Talking problems through is important, but spontaneity and humor are two major elements of any successful relationship. "Comic relief" can't make a problem go away, but it can open up the doors of communication for later discussion. Also, light-hearted play is definitely erotic, and can lead to some of the best sensual experiences you'll have together. We're firm believers in the idea that good sexual communication is one of the major elements of a committed relationship. Feel free to suspend intensity and have fun!

Exercise 6. Take a Vacation from Your Problems. Go out to dinner and talk about the good times you've had together. Tell each other what your happiest moments together have been, and think aloud about those times when you seemed to achieve the perfect equation—just the right amount of intimacy. If this sort of "vacation" works well for you, plan to take a similar "vacation" together every week. You can also talk about why you were originally attracted to one another; this is a good reminder for the man who defends against intimacy by criticizing a woman for the very things that once won him.

We often ask couples to describe a period in their relationship when they felt the most loved. When we asked Cheryl and Dave to recall this time in their lives, Cheryl told us without a moment's hesitation that it was the time when she'd been severely depressed and Dave's nurturing instincts had been mobilized by the crisis. "So," we said, somewhat ironically, "now that you aren't depressed anymore and you have a great career, do you have to give it all up to save the relationship?" They both laughed, but it was an important lesson for them.

Apparently, Dave could only give to Cheryl when she was a vegetable and he was in total control. (Unconsciously, Cheryl knew that the only way that Dave would tune in was if she fell apart.) What to do? First of all, Cheryl had to let him know that she was neither a basket case nor a perfectly self-sufficient automaton. She shouldn't wait till she was desperate to let him know what her specific needs were. And then, of course, Dave had to learn the signals and respond *before* she fell apart. A small adjustment, such as this, can break a dangerous pattern.

Exercise 7. Don't Have Sex—Unless You Love It. When a couple comes to therapy and tells us that sex is no good because the man has become withdrawn, controlling, sadistic, or just mechanical, the first thing we tell them is "no sex." In other words, don't continue to have an unsatisfying sexual relationship. You don't have to be a therapist to say this: if you aren't having fun with sex, stop.

Ways to Get a Man to Give Sexually

Once you have stopped having sex, you can go back to square one and start giving and getting pleasure. When a man withdraws from sex or is overly controlling, he is fearful of giving "too much" to a woman (if he gives to her, he fears that he will lose himself). Other men don't want to give—period. They just don't see what's in it for them. These exercises are not about performance or technique: they are designed to take the pressure off both of you and help a man learn to give.

1. Fantasize. If he's been withdrawn or controlling, turn back the clock to the days when you were still hot for each other. Remembering the lust and romance will surround each of you with a new sexual aura. Tell each other your fantasies in person or on the phone, *but don't act on them.* Rent a sexy movie and watch it together on the VCR; read good porn to each other (Anaïs Nin, for example, has two collections of terrific, sensual, sexy stories; often, women's erotica is the sexiest of all). Make it a game: How sexy can you get without ripping off each other's clothes and falling into bed? The key to this exercise is: don't *do* anything—*yet.*

2. Everything-But-Intercourse Exercises. This involves giving and taking sensual, *but not sexual,* pleasure. Leisurely caressing, without any "goal" except the mutual enjoyment of one another's bodies, is the gateway to great sex. This is a real test for many men who are stuck with commitment issues; a man may not want to take the time to give pleasure to his partner. The benefit of this exercise is not only in doing it, but in seeing how each of you *reacts* to doing it. For him, giving pleasure may mean "giving in" to you or giving up control to you; it may mean simply that he is accustomed to having it all *his* way, or that sex, for him, is simply a matter of getting off and getting it over with. When this exercise works to your mutual satisfaction, go on to genital massage; then mutual orgasms without intercourse; and finally, intercourse.

Here's another suggestion: Let's say that each of you has agreed to be "in charge" on alternate nights (usually the person who is scheduled to "get" is the one who must make sure the tryst takes place). If Tuesday is his night, for example, he gets to choose the place, the time, the position. On your night, the same rules apply. This is an excellent (and exciting) exercise for people learning how to take control—or give it up. If he has a problem giving to you in other ways (see Exercises 1 and 3) *you will experience the problem most intensely in bed.* Finally, if his problem is and continues to be across the board, he's probably a Good For Nothing Guy, and an all-round bad bet.

Relationship Workouts

Let's say you've tried all the exercises we've described—and things still aren't working out. Stronger measures are called for.

1. The Ultimatum. Ann and Jerry had been together for two years. They were close enough to Level Four, Monogamy Plus, for Ann to want Jerry to move in with her. For months, he stalled and pondered until Ann thought she was going crazy. Finally, she looked at her watch and said, "You have exactly forty-eight hours to decide."

Ann had a feeling the "Do it or else" tactic would work. You have to be confident that it *will* work—a man should be close enough to making the decision himself that all he needs is a nudge. Another woman gave a man six months to decide if they'd live together (the subject had been under lengthy discussion and the level of commitment they'd reached matched her demand). And another woman who had lived with her boyfriend for several years finally decided that she needed a more formalized commitment. She told him she wanted to know within three months whether or not the marriage was on. Finally, only half-jokingly, she literally twisted his arm behind his back one day and said, "Okay! This is it! Will you marry me or not?" All of these men rose to the ultimatums women put to them. But if you do give a man an ultimatum, know clearly that he is at the same advanced level of commitment that you are. If you aren't, this tactic will backfire. (Also, once you've given an ultimatum, you can't back down and say you were just kidding. It's no joke—you've defined the bottom line for yourself.)

A different kind of ultimatum that we sometimes recommend to women is a secret one, which is useful at a lower level of commitment. Let's say a woman has tried talking about her lack of sexual gratification with her boyfriend. She has also initiated sensual exercises, but she's frustrated; every time it's his turn to give to her, he's resentful. She hates the way he slaps cream on her back and mechanically rubs it in—he's so impersonal, she'd be better off getting a massage at the health club!

If our sexual relationship doesn't improve in three months, she decides, I'm calling it quits. She feels better immediately. When a woman has her own timetable, she has a sense of control; she defines her needs and makes her own decisions. She doesn't have the sinking feeling that it's all in his hands.

Ultimatums are particularly useful for women feeling time pressure. If you're 35, and you're with a man who can't commit to making any plans beyond next weekend, think seriously either about laying it on the line to him or having your own secret timetable. You'll know which is appropriate to your own situation.

2. The Temporary Separation.   When your fights are endless, repetitive, and wearisome (like a load of dirty wash that keeps recycling), a week away from one another can purge the rage and bad feelings you both have. It's a relief to stop fighting, which can make you so crazy you hardly recognize yourself anymore. (Or him; instead of being your lover, he's now become your torturer.) A separation can also help you reaffirm yourself as an individual who can live without this relationship. As one woman put it: "I realized I could live without him. I spent the week seeing friends, going to movies, reading books, going to bed, and eating dinner whenever I felt like it. By the time I saw him again, I felt like I'd spent a month at a spa."

Discuss the separation in advance with your partner and decide the terms (will you have phone conversations or go completely cold turkey?). Try to plan something special to do when you have your "first date." Couples often feel more appreciative of one another after a separation; a short hiatus can help you remember that you actually liked this person at one time.

3. Seeing Other People.   Up until Level Three, monogamy, we absolutely encourage women to play the field. Don't sit around waiting for a man to call you—dress up and go out. That's probably what *he's* doing. One woman client was dating several men at one time but having sex with only one of them. Did this mean she should drop the others and be monogamous? she wanted to know. She was so obviously reluctant to do so that we advised her to keep it light with the first guy and keep seeing the others until she knew which one to choose. If you drop phone-sitting from your repertoire and have fun instead, your self-esteem will soar so high you'll hardly recognize it.

Seeing other people once you are monogamous is a different matter. You may have agreed to monogamy too fast or too soon, and it isn't going as you want it to. Barry refuses to account for his time to Andrea, even though they see one another exclusively and *appear* to have reached the third level of commitment. He also expects her to drop everything the minute he calls. Acquiescing to this made her feel as if she were 16, mooning around at home and waiting for the captain of the football team to call. "I've outgrown this stuff," she told herself. "Why should he have all the pieces on *his* side of the board?" She told Barry that she thought they'd moved ahead too quickly, and that it would be best for both of them to date other people.

Andrea and Barry agreed to backtrack to Level Two. This didn't mean they'd decided to break up—just lighten up. After

Andrea took charge of the situation, she went out and bought herself a dress she'd had her eye on for weeks and had lunch with a man in her office who attracted her. "I'm not waiting for Barry," she says. "If he thinks it over and decides to work things out with me, great. If he doesn't, then I'll know he isn't right for me."

Don't think of this as a tactic to get a man "to come around" and see things your way; think of it as a way to build your self-respect and enjoy yourself. Sometimes a man will suggest "seeing other people," and you suspect that he really is trying to break up with you. Don't say yes and then sit at home and wait for him to call. Let your friends know you're looking, and forget about him.

If All Else Fails

Let's say you just can't hack it. You're both too angry, too resentful, too enmeshed, to be objective. You've talked about "the relationship" until it's a third party—between you, you've created a Frankenstein's monster that won't give you any peace. It's bigger, stronger, and nastier than you are, and *it* is in charge. To get back in control it makes sense to hire a therapist for guidance and assistance. A therapist can help you work it out or break it off. (Remember: A therapist won't figure out the problems for you—she'll help *you* figure it out and make your own decision.)

"I can't believe I actually agreed to marry this guy," Laura said. "I feel like I never want to see him again."

Over the phone her voice shook with angry tears. Laura and Eric had had their first couples therapy session earlier in the day—and it had been a shocker for Laura. Ever since they'd been engaged, Eric had acted like a different person, she told us, and the session had confirmed to her that she was living with a Dr. Jekyll and Mr. Hyde. After the couple had set a wedding date and ordered the invitations, Laura moved into Eric's apartment. Suddenly, he'd wanted her to sign a prenuptial agreement, itemizing everything, from his assets to how many times he'd agree to see her parents every year (never mentioning *his* parents). He also wouldn't allow her to move in any of her furniture (he didn't like her taste) and complained bitterly when she put her leather pocketbook on his favorite upholstered chair (it would ruin the fabric, he claimed). During the session Laura had been amazed to hear that Eric considered her a slob, irresponsible, and not on par intellectually and esthetically with his life-style. She'd also found out, to her horror, that Eric's last relationship had gone the same way. He'd been happily engaged, then had suddenly begun to find fault with his fiancée. Eventually, she'd walked out on him.

Now, on the phone, she said, "I think I still love him, but I don't know—he hardly seems like the same guy! Don't you think his problems are just too extreme?"

"He does seem to have a strong reaction to getting married," we agreed cautiously, "but it seems to us that Eric has the same problems a lot of men are having."

"I don't know if I want to go through with either the therapy or the relationship," she said.

"Let's raise these questions in your next session," we told her, wary of setting up an alliance with her against Eric. Nothing could be more destructive to the therapy.

But Laura was too upset to get off the phone right away. "This could get worse after we get married!" she said. "I'm only twenty-eight, this isn't the end of the line for me. I'm not desperate, I want a lot of really wonderful things in my life."

"The fact that he is willing to come to therapy with you is a positive sign," we told her.

"He wouldn't have come at all if I hadn't dragged him out of the apartment!"

"Well, that was just the first time," we said. "The first time is always hard for both members of a couple. Now he's agreed to put out the time and money and energy. He's agreed to work on the relationship. Let's talk about all of your doubts in the session."

Laura took a deep breath and agreed to continue with the short-term couples therapy she and Eric had undertaken.

Couples Therapy—When Should You Go?

Obviously, if you are at any of the pre-monogamous levels of commitment, couples therapy is not an option. As we told Laura, the very act of going to see a therapist together assumes a minimal mutual commitment. There are two basic situations that might send you as a couple into therapy. First, like Laura and Eric, you might find that your relationship is in a sudden, serious crisis; in this case Eric began acting "out of character," or "not like himself," as Laura put it. In fact, Eric was behaving in classic Good Guy Today/Gone Tomorrow style. Fearing loss of control, he imposed a cold, impersonal prenuptial agreement upon her; then, in a cold sweat at the prospect of her moving in and taking over his life, he accused her of being a slob. Eric had drummed up all of the familiar male defenses to help relieve his anxiety.

The other situation that may send a couple to a therapist is the chronic, stalled-out, going-nowhere relationship, in which they are constantly taking one step forward and two steps backward. The perfect example is the couple whose sex life is fine until they begin spending lots of time together and feel very close. They back off, sex improves; they begin to get close again, sex goes cold and flat as last night's champagne. Meanwhile, frustration grows. A therapist may be able to help by pointing out the pattern of behavior and what the behavior means.

Why He Will Resist Going

You say, "Let's go to a therapist!" He says, "Let's go skiing!" His secret fear is that the therapist will be on your side, and that she will "pry things out of him" that he doesn't want to share. He resents the idea of handing over control to someone else (or so it seems to him) just so that he can end up seeing himself in a bad light! For these reasons a man may say to you, "Therapy is a waste of time and money." Or he'll suddenly become very judgmental and say, "If we can't solve our *own* problems, something is really wrong with us." Often, however, men end up loving therapy so much they become therapy-promoters and start referring their friends in droves. For a man, therapy can be freeing; suddenly, he discovers a whole new dimension of himself—the dimension of feelings. This can be pretty heady stuff.

Four Ways to Get a Man to Try Therapy

1. Tell him he only has to try it once.
2. Tell him to do it "for you." A man may feel that even though he obviously has no problems, *you* certainly do. (Don't worry—once you get him to the office, this delusion will be quickly dispelled.)
3. Tell him that he can choose the therapist.
4. Dare him. "Don't be scared—come on!" This is a challenge he may be unable to resist.

How Long Will it Take?

Boosting a couple over a hurdle, getting a read-out, and/or going on to the next level of commitment will take up to three months. In this time, a therapist should be able to identify patterns and defenses and see on which level of commitment the problems started. (The other form of couples therapy, which usually involves married couples who want to improve their relationship, may take up to a year.) But at three months, sometimes less, you can find out what you need to know, which is whether the relationship is worth working on. To help Laura and Eric decide, we recommended shifting into reverse, temporarily shelving the wedding plans, chalking up the cost of the invitations as a loss, and taking time out for three months to evaluate themselves as a couple. The problems may turn out to be too extreme, as Laura fears; by the end of three months she'll know for sure.

How to Choose a Couples Therapist

The best route to follow here is word of mouth: Talk to friends who've seen couples therapists and get the lowdown from them; a trustworthy friend's good experience with a therapist is probably the best recommendation you can get. Or, ask a mental health professional for referrals.

Since couples therapy is not a long-term proposition, the emotional hookup between you and the therapist should be quick. Both you and your partner should walk out of that first session with the sense that the therapist has understood *both* of you—and put both of you on the spot (at least a little). Within three sessions, at the most, you have a perfect right to expect to learn from your therapist: 1) what the major issues of the relationship are; 2) how long the therapy will likely take; and 3) what you can hope to accomplish within this time frame.

If a therapist doesn't answer these questions, be wary! You *do* deserve answers—that's what couples therapy is for.

Exercises to help a relationship that's not going anywhere:

- Do something nice for each other once a day, and write it down. *Don't tell* your partner what you did for him until later; then, discuss it.
- Be selfish once a day—choose one thing you really want to do for yourself. Encourage your partner to do the same.
- Spend some time apart—it's okay to pull back when you need to.
- The Talking Cure: one partner talks about his/her feelings for fifteen minutes straight; the other partner listens. Then the roles are reversed. Each *must talk* about feelings and each *must listen.*
- Don't forget to "play." The fun activities that you did when you first started dating (tennis, dancing, and so on) should continue to be a part of the relationship.
- Take a vacation from your problems—declare a "truce" and have an evening when they're forgotten for the moment.
- If sex is no longer fun, *stop.* Don't resume until some of the problems within the relationship begin to be worked out. You may, however, enjoy sensual activities other than intercourse which can be mutually pleasing and satisfying.

If the above strategies don't work, proceed to stronger measures:

- Deliver an ultimatum with a time limit attached.
- Pick a time frame in the near future (two–four months) during which you will decide if he is capable of commitment. You need not share this time frame with him. If at the end of this period he has made little or no progress, move on.
- Enforce a temporary separation until you can talk less emotionally.
- As a way to regain your self-respect as well as to have fun, see other men.
- Couples therapy—get him to go to a therapist with you.

8

Baby Fever

Once upon a time, not so long ago, women married young and had babies (they didn't necessarily live happily ever after, but that's not the way the story went). Blank stares would have greeted any mention of a "biological clock." But now that people date for years before they marry, many women are ending up in the cruelest crunch of all. A woman in her thirties, who has always felt that she had the luxury of time, may suddenly feel as if she has to meet the right man, get married, and get pregnant *today.* She's in a dead heat with her body and with time, which is not only gaining on her but breathing down her neck. She feels she can't mess up, can't waste a minute, can't make a mistake. It's the worst kind of deadline.

This is all bad enough. But if you add to the biological clock men's problems with commitment, you've got the perfect double whammy for women. If women don't automatically assume that most men will dawdle, balk, and drag their feet through the levels of commitment—while others don't move at all—it is all too easy to end up desperate. We tell all of our women clients: "You can't wait longer and trust that everything will fall into place. It won't." At the same time we say: "It isn't your fault!" By portraying single women in their thirties as poor, sad creatures (beneath their high-powered, career-oriented exteriors), the media has often made women feel that by "waiting too long," they blew it. *Any* woman can get married, if that's her goal—but today's woman is *not* desperate for marriage. She's desperate for a *good* marriage.

To avoid the Big Crunch, you have to be smart about yourself and about men. Since the early 1970s the trend has been to blur the differences between men and women, which has helped women begin to catch up with men in the career arena. But women and men *are* different in one major respect: women bear the burden of biology—as well as the weight of cultural disapproval if they "end up" unmarried and childless.

If you do want to get married and have children, you need to become more analytical about men earlier on. If you do want children, don't let a relationship with a man who doesn't want them drag on for years. You should be able to find out by the time you're at Level Two, that of steady dating, what his general idea of the future is. (And at this point, keep it general; you don't necessarily want him to marry you, you just want a sense of who he is and what he wants.)

Lots of couples in their thirties come to us for treatment because the woman, acutely aware of the demands of time and her body, feels the need to kick the relationship up one notch or several. Suddenly, then, the couple is up against a wall: What for *her* is a natural and necessary move elicits in *him* an overwhelming desire to take the back door out. Some men can and will adjust to a woman's agenda; others can't—and won't.

At age 38, Claire wanted to have a baby. She'd felt the urge before but never this powerfully, and now she was beginning to wonder if it would ever happen. Her boyfriend, Tom, was several years younger and indifferent to babies; whenever they spent time with married friends of hers who had children, she'd catch him tapping his foot and checking his watch. When she asked him how he felt about kids, he'd always give a joking, noncommittal reply: Kids were terrific—*other* people's kids. Claire said nothing to him about her own feelings; instead, she became more and more depressed; sometimes, she said, she woke up in the middle of the night, thinking, "Oh my God, I'm going to miss my chance. In a few years I'll be too old to have a baby." Worse, she was in love with Tom. She didn't want to have just any baby; she wanted to have *their* baby.

One day her friend Margo said casually, "Maybe if you got pregnant, things would speed up." They discussed a couple they knew who got married after the woman became pregnant. "It all worked out for them," Claire concluded thoughtfully. She also decided to discuss it with Tom; once he understood why she should really have a baby *now,* he'd be likely to agree to it. (Wouldn't he? After all, the two of them had been seeing each other for a couple of years and were actually very close.) But when she finally did bring up her desire to have a child, he cringed and said, "I don't think I'm ready for this."

Strangely, as if she'd had a green light from Tom, Claire's heart soared. He hadn't hit the ceiling, she reasoned; he hadn't fainted; and he hadn't walked out on her. Blithely, she interpreted his response as "Maybe I'm not ready now, but I will be ready soon." This is it! she exulted. I'll get pregnant and then we'll get married!

Confidently, she put away her diaphragm, without telling Tom. Claire was so happy that she didn't make much of the fact that he was often withdrawn, even sullen. "He'll feel better when all of this is settled," she assured herself. But a few months later, when she raced to the phone to tell him the news of her pregnancy, she was greeted by a dead, heavy silence on the other end of the phone. Then Tom told her that he didn't want to get married and he didn't want to have a baby. Not only that but he felt duped, betrayed by Claire's pregnancy. He'd never agreed to it in the first place!

Claire was furious. *He* felt duped—*he* felt betrayed! What about *her?* "Are you in or out?" she asked him. "I'm confused" he replied. So why hadn't he told her how he felt in the first place? she asked. He *had* told her, Tom insisted stubbornly. She just hadn't listened. Claire took a deep breath. "All right," she said. "Then I'll have an abortion." When Tom said nothing, she knew that all of her plans—and her pregnancy—were finished.

Your time and pacing should no more dominate a relationship than a man's should. Claire's feelings and fantasies are completely understandable, but her reading of the relationship could not have been more cockeyed. It was, in fact, purely wishful thinking. Tom was nowhere near being able to make a commitment, but she interpreted his "I'm not ready" as "I'll *get* ready." No way. Tom was so much *not* ready that he became a victim of his own wishful thinking, too. "If I ignore this whole thing, maybe it'll go away," he thought. And he continued his sexual relationship with Claire as if their conversation had never happened.

In a few years, Tom may be Good Enough and good and ready to make a commitment to, and a baby with, a woman. A Good Enough Guy who is scared (most men will be) but who could be ready anyway, will tell a woman who wants a baby, "I don't know. Let's talk about it." This is the kind of talk that flows out of a sense of mutual commitment; in fact, no couple should discuss pregnancy until they have reached the fourth level of Monogamy Plus and are planning for a shared future. Before this, you can feel out a man's general attitude toward marriage and children, if that's what your goal is. But don't get ahead of yourself. When he says he isn't ready, believe it.

The Baby—Or Him?

In the four years that 40-year-old Gayle has lived with Patrick she has become pregnant twice "accidentally." Now she is trying to decide whether or not to have a second abortion. Patrick has told her he does not want a child, and even though he won't stand in her way if she wants to go through with the pregnancy, he will not help her, either. Gayle interprets her "accidental" pregnancies as proof of her deep desire to have a child. And yet, here she is, living with a man who has no interest in a family. She senses that if she decides to have the baby, Patrick will leave her. It is the worst dilemma of her life—the baby or Patrick?

Maybe if she went ahead and had the baby, Patrick would come around. She's heard of such things happening, but somehow she doesn't believe Patrick would. In his forties, Patrick is still just barely scraping by as an actor and is still talking about his need for "space." He gets glassy-eyed whenever she talks about marriage; by now, all of her friends have advised her to leave him.

She's thought about it. And *thought* about it. But she feels that she's invested an enormous amount in her relationship with Patrick. There is a shared network of friends, wonderful vacations together, a familiarity of routine, and a strong, intimate friendship with Patrick's older sister. It all seems too much to give up, so Gayle has always decided against leaving Patrick—and now she decides not to rock the boat. She has her second abortion, aware that this will probably be her last pregnancy, and her last chance to have a child.

But afterward, Gayle is still haunted by the question of whether she should hang in a relationship in which she is not getting what she wanted. No baby, no marriage—is it worth it?

If a man has trouble breathing in a relationship—if, for him, two is already a crowd—a woman can't expect him to welcome a third person into his already-threatened psychic space. Even though Gayle and Patrick have been living together for years, they never resolved the earlier stages of the relationship. If you are in this dilemma, read about the levels of commitment again and determine honestly where you stand by thinking about his behavior and realizing where *he* fits on the commitment scale. In Gayle's case, this might be as good as the relationship will get; at this point, with so much time and energy put in, she will probably stay with what she has.

Making a Baby

If you are living with a man or have been monogamous for a while but are not sure of your true level of commitment, you can be sure that a man will show his true colors around the issue of your biological clock. If he acts put upon and says, "If I hear 'biological clock' one more time, I'll flip," or mutters resentfully, "I'm at the mercy of *her* biological clock," watch out. If you talk about having a baby and he makes you feel as if you are gripped in the hysterical throes of your hormones, don't think you can count on him. And if he acts as if he's never heard of sex for anything except recreation, don't expect a libidinal about-face.

A man should not be made to feel you are using him as a stud service, but at a certain stage in the relationship, he should certainly see your baby urge as an issue that concerns both of you. At the level of Monogamy Plus, you aren't socking him with an inappropriate issue if you talk about having a baby. In fact, now that you're talking about a shared future, it's inappropriate to avoid it. But realize that you should expect some problems at *any* level.

Robert, 40, has lived with Rosemary for three years, and now that she is 39 and wants a child, he has finally (after months of discussion) agreed to it. But it hasn't been so easy for Rosemary to get pregnant. Every month, she takes her basal body temperature and carefully records it on a chart to determine the days of maximum fertility. For a couple of months, her temperature indicated that she hadn't ovulated, and she got very depressed.

But for the past two months it has risen, and now she sees a pattern so that this month she has been able to pinpoint the exact day when they should have sex. She is high with excitement—this will be the month it happens, she's sure of it!

It is the fateful morning. "I don't feel like it," Robert says, yawning.

"What do you mean you don't *feel* like it?" Rosemary asks him, sitting bolt upright in bed.

Well . . . he's tired. He has too much on his mind. He has a meeting at work in an hour.

Rosemary lies in bed contemplating murder. With Robert dead, she could sign up for artificial insemination—a way to get pregnant that was obviously a whole lot easier and simpler than dealing with a man.

When Rosemary and Robert come to our office for a session later that same day, Rosemary is still livid—and Robert still unmoved.

"I just didn't *feel* like having sex this morning," he says.

"Do you think *I* feel like having sex according to a chart?" Rosemary asks him. "Of course I don't! But this isn't even about sex, it's about having a baby, and you agreed to it!"

"I don't like being told what to do," Robert says. "I hate authority."

"What do you think this is—1967?" Rosemary explodes. "We're not free spirits and hippies anymore. It's 19*87!*"

We said that if Robert were really committed to her (and he was), he'd have to conform to the regimen they'd agreed on together. But why had he suddenly balked? Throughout their relationship, Robert has had some familiar male troubles. He feels entitled to his moods; for example, if he doesn't feel like talking at dinner, he clams up, leaving Rosemary to pick up the slack. It's difficult for him, as it is for many men, to subordinate his own individual needs, desires, and impulses to what is good for the relationship. He feels a threat to his sense of freedom, even his sense of self.

"I didn't feel like going to see your mother in the hospital the other day," Rosemary tells him. "I hate hospitals! But I went anyway. I did it for her and for you and for the two of us. Sometimes you have to."

Robert gritted his teeth and agreed to the sex-by-chart regimen. In this case, Rosemary was right to push; reluctant and ambivalent as Robert may be sometimes, he is willing and committed most of the time. Not pushing him would have brought them no closer to having a baby than Claire and Tom are. But unlike Claire, Rosemary was in a situation in which a good push was sure to bring results.

Do You Want His Genes?

Shortly after Marian broke up with Seth, she discussed with family and friends the possibility of artificial insemination. She was 37 and felt ready, emotionally and financially, to have a child. The break-up with Seth had been long and painful; in this case Seth had wanted to get married but Marian had never felt sure enough. He often seemed to her to be childish and dependent; of the two of them, she alone was established in her career and home (by the age of 38, he'd changed careers several times.) At first, Seth had kept his distance from her; then, he began to seem too needy. He was always showing up at her apartment, assuming she wanted to see him. Gradually, more and more of his clothes, records, and books were accumulating in piles in the corners. If she let him, Marian realized, this man would move into her life—permanently. He would probably become her husband and the father of her children.

The idea gave her goose bumps. She didn't love him, didn't want him in those roles. She did, however, want a child. Accustomed to independence and self-sufficiency, Marian thought about her options. She made a good salary and had a close family and friends. She knew that if she decided to have a child on her own, everyone would support her. Finally, she broke up with Seth, and several months later, made her decision to be artificially inseminated. "Having a child doesn't mean I've given up on having a relationship with a man someday," she says. "But if a man is turned off by a child in my life, I wouldn't want to be with him anyway!"

For a woman who doesn't feel that marriage is a necessity, it is liberating to know that childbearing is still very much within her power to choose. "My body was telling me," Marian says, " 'If you want to have a baby, you'd better do it soon.' It was good to know it was *my* option, my decision." However, a woman should know who she is and what she wants before making this decision—being a mother is hard enough; being a single mother takes a special passion and a special sort of strength. Even when you are unmarried and pushing the deadline, this decision is more likely *not* to be right for you.

It wasn't for Miranda. "I wanted a child," she says, "but in my heart I knew it wasn't right for me. I'm settled; I have my routines, my work, my friends. A baby would shell shock my life; I'd go broke and I'd feel overwhelmed with responsibility. I checked it out with my accountant, and he told me a baby would cost me $10,000 every year; I'd have to take a second job, and I'd never see the baby anyway!" She also valued her freedom and personal mobility too much to want to be confined to a small apartment and a demanding infant. The antibaby decision was painful, but she could only go on what was right for her; where another woman might see a challenge, Miranda knew she'd be snowed under.

Happiness doesn't have to do with being married or not being married. A woman who is 40 and not married hasn't eliminated the possibility of long-term relationships from her life. The difficulty is giving up the traditional trappings you'd always thought you'd have—and redefining yourself. Up until your late twenties you had a bead on yourself as a young career woman with plenty of boyfriends who would someday marry and have children. Suddenly, the gears grind and shift—you wake up one day and you look in the mirror and see a single woman in her middle thirties. She is *you*. And it's a shock. Whether you were consciously aware of it or not, you'd envisioned sharing your life with a man. You still might—but your arrangements might be unconventional (we know couples who are committed to one another but don't live together, for example; we also know women who have more than one ongoing, long-term relationship—so your options are as good as your imagination).

One woman says that in her family single women were considered to be pathetic creatures known as "spinsters" and "old maids." They didn't get married because nobody asked them. In her family's eyes, she is a spinster. But is she really a wizened old crone? Hardly. She's dated a lot and could have gotten married several times, if marriage were her goal. But she's haunted by the specter of the spinster: for the past several months she's stayed in a second-rate relationship in which there is companionship but little passion. She stays in it because she has the gnawing sense that this is "the best I can do." It *isn't*. The relationship serves as a "safe house" refuge against unknown possibilities—until the day she's ready to step out into uncharted territory.

For now, though, she feels that for her, marriage and children just wasn't "meant to be"—meaning that it isn't in her stars. In this mystical point of view lurks an insidious sense of failure, a belief that while the goodies were being handed out, she'd been overlooked. But do *single men* consider themselves failures? Quite the opposite! They're practically our national heroes! In our culture it is assumed that the single guy is a free spirit who has chosen the unencumbered life—but women don't choose, goes the popular wisdom, they miss out.

Caroline, 40, happily single and childless, is living disproof of this nonsense. In group therapy with six other people, all (unhappily) married, Caroline feels no unbearable itch to marry. If the right man came along, certainly she'd go for it. A few years ago she was in a relationship that left her shaken and wounded. Her lover lied to her, betrayed her in countless ways, and sleazed out of every minor commitment he made to her. Afterward, she was convinced for a while that it was too late for her (she was 37), and that she would never find the right man (*"Not* Mr. Right," she says, "I never believed in him; I just wanted mutual respect and love"). She recovered from the trauma and is now in a relationship that satisfies her. She and her lover see one another only on weekends, when they do something special—theater or a concert—and spend the rest of the time in bed. The separation during the week adds an exciting, anticipatory edge to sex. Caroline thrives on the excitement and passion, the sense that there is something illicit about their weekends at home in bed and in secluded country inns. She has no desire to up the level of commitment; why change her life now, she asks, when she has a great sex life, work she loves, friends she adores, and a million other activities?

One day, in a group session, Caroline asked: "Is there something wrong with me because I'm *not* unhappy? *Shouldn't* I be unhappy?" Everyone laughed, but then took her questions seriously. The point is that Caroline *is* happy; her only problem is the expectations other people (and society) have of her. Without that burden (she worries that her mother will be disappointed if she doesn't marry, for example), Caroline's life is satisfying. "So why are you in group therapy?" someone asked. "You're the healthiest person among all of us!" Caroline hesitated before answering, then said, "I love this group. All of you are important people in my life."

If someday she does marry, Caroline would prefer a divorced man who has children of his own. She'd like to have children in her life, she says, but doesn't have a craving to have her *own* children. (Since many women *don't* feel this way about "other people's children," she has something special to offer a divorced man.) But all in all, the issue for Caroline is to have deep connections with other people in her life, not to get married at all costs.

It is just as important to get your career in order as it is to have a relationship. But most of us are capable of doing both—and that's the great thing about women; women *are* able to handle lots of things going on in their lives at once. Don't let time tyrannize you, but do think about it now, whatever your age. An older woman has the advantage of knowing clearly what she wants and cutting through bad relationships more quickly. A younger woman can get wise faster. "I know what I want," says Louise, 29. "So, when I go out with a man, I'm straight about the fact that I'm not playing around, and that I'm looking for a serious relationship. Wally was taken aback when I told him this, but then he said he wanted it, too. Will we end up getting married and living happily ever after? I don't know, but I don't want to waste time anymore with men who don't have the same goals I have."

You don't have all the time in the world if you want to have children. This isn't a tragedy—it just means you need to have a little extra self-awareness. Louise is right: the important thing is to know who you are and what you want.

First, you shouldn't expect a man who's not at least at Level Four, Monogamy Plus, to consider having a child. You cannot force him to skip a stage because of your biological clock; on the other hand, be aware of your time limits. He may think he wants a child, or he may come right out and say he doesn't. The following are signs that he is not ready for fatherhood:

- He helps you plot your temperature chart for fertility but then becomes disinterested in sex on the very days you're most fertile. (Here, you need to confront him with his mixed signals.)
- He enjoys your friends' children but balks whenever you bring up how much you'd like to have your own.
- He complains to his friends, "I'm at the mercy of *her* biological clock."
- You've been living together for five years, and you're both in your mid-thirties. You want children; he doesn't even want to discuss getting married. (In this situation you need to think about calling it quits—see chapter 10.)
- He says he loves children and wants them—someday. He's in his late twenties and you're turning thirty in a few months. Somehow you suspect he's not talking about having children with *you,* he's probably a Good Enough Guy, but it's just too early for him.

9

In Name Only:
When Marriage Doesn't
Equal Commitment

Is a man cured of commitment problems the day he slips on a wedding ring? Can you sit back and breathe a sigh of relief? *Don't* sit back; marriage is a minefield.

Many women find that husbands have even more problems with intimacy than boyfriends do. After a man has committed to marriage, his old fear of intimacy may rear its ugly head; at this point a woman may feel as if she would have been better off single (and still hoping). "When we got married, I thought we'd solved all our problems," says Jan, "but our first year of marriage was hell. It turned out to be the hardest time we'd ever spent together." When intimacy on a daily basis becomes the regular menu, a man may backslide in any number of unexpected ways. "I took the big step," one man said. "But now if I can't go out with my friends three or four nights a week, I feel trapped." His wife says she doesn't mind, but she does. She knows that even though he loves her, deep down he hasn't given her his heart.

Deep down, then, are most married men still bachelors?

Many men in the Good Guy Today/Gone Tomorrow category unconsciously fear that by getting married they will "become" their fathers, that beast of burden who was "chained to the family" and dogged by responsibility. Most women don't demand this of their husbands, but they *are* demanding intimacy—over the long haul, every day, and in many ways.

A Marriage Horror Story

In the weeks after the ceremony, Greg began to act as if he hated his wife. He refused to hold her hand, kiss her, make love with her, or even return her phone calls when she tried to reach him at work. Margery was stunned; she'd assumed Greg's problems with commitment were finished on the day he'd given her a big, glittering diamond engagement ring. The fact is, Greg hadn't been ready for marriage at all—his actual level of commitment had never surpassed steady dating (when they were supposedly monogamous, he'd actually been going out to bars and picking up women for one-night stands). But because Margery wanted it so much, eventually he'd gotten swept up in Marriage Fever (several of his best friends also got married in a matter of months). But when the fever cooled down, the marriage died with a whimper—and a year later, almost to the day, Margery walked out. "Be careful what you ask for," she says wryly. "You may get what you want."

Pushing a man through the levels of commitment and into marriage is disastrous, but if you don't skip steps there's no reason to fear that your husband will turn into your worst enemy. (Usually, a Good For Nothing Guy like Greg doesn't make it anywhere near an altar or a judge.) But many men in the middle category of Good Guy Today will use various means to shore up against intimacy when they marry. (Research has shown that men don't become "affiliative" until they're in their fifties, while for women in their thirties, the need for connection presses hard. The timing is off; a married man in his thirties is a slow learner because intimacy simply is not yet on his agenda.) What we're going to talk about now are a few of the most common symptoms of cold feet you'll find in a married man (and what to do about them).

1. He'll dump the housework on you.

Even a man who, before marriage, was big on sharing equally in household tasks (and considered it ideologically correct to do so and even castigated other men for opting out) may suddenly forget how to wash a dish. If he does, he's trying to exercise a time-honored male privilege, and it's more than laziness—it's a commitment issue.

When Jan and Peter got married, their friends rejoiced. Over the course of five years, the relationship had careened into dead-ends, collided into brick walls, and overturned in ditches. Each time, they picked themselves up and (shakily) got back together again. As a typical Good Guy Today/Gone Tomorrow, Peter had wanted Jan to be his equal intellectually and professionally— he'd talked a great game about equality. At the same he always wanted her to be available when he needed her and to pick up all the slack in the relationship (the way he expected her to pick up the clothes he dropped on the floor). He'd expect her to wait up for him when he was late coming home, but wouldn't dream of doing the same for her. Jan also usually ended up cooking most of their dinners and cleaning up afterward. Before they got married, she made it clear that she wouldn't put up with this. Peter agreed that it was positively medieval of him to expect her to.

One week after the wedding, Jan, who had a demanding sixty-hour-a-week job, found that she was doing all the housework. She talked to Peter about it—why was he backsliding on their former decision to share the misery? "I don't want a relationship where I'm doing everything," she told him firmly. Peter gulped and said, "Gee, I'm sorry," and promised to do better. He "did better" for two days.

And so it went for months and months. Endless talking led to endless migraines. "You're a nag," Peter told her, which made Jan cringe, but she stuck to her guns anyway. Finally, in sheer exasperation, Jan took her pillow and blanket and made up a bed for herself in the living room. She would not, she said, move back into bed with Peter until he shaped up. A few days later, Peter quietly began picking up around the house, cooking, and shopping. Even after Jan moved back into the bedroom, he gritted his teeth and stuck to it.

The first years of marriage are always tough; this is the time when you're laying the foundation for what you've decided is a lifetime commitment. When Peter wouldn't keep up his end of the relationship, Jan felt as if he weren't thinking of the two of them—only of himself. She couldn't feel close to him unless they were sharing the unpleasant tasks. When Peter opted out, she felt as if he were opting out of the relationship; she felt as if he considered her time less important than his, and that she (like her mother) was going to spend her life like a human vacuum cleaner, picking up after him. When talking didn't help, she realized that dramatic action was in order.

We strongly recommend taking action—in a situation such as this, sleep in the living room or go to a motel. Or, on the night he has his boss over to dinner, "forget" to clean the toilet or to take out the overflowing bags of garbage. Or, if he isn't doing the laundry the way he agreed to, buy lots of underpants and settle in for a long siege (he'll get around to it). Or, you might dress up like a maid and hand him a bill at the end of the week. Use your imagination, try different strategies—don't give up till *something* works. Jan made her point in a way that touched Peter where it really hurt: he'd rather scrub the kitchen floor with a toothbrush than give up having her warm body beside him in bed.

When you are married, the stakes are higher, and there's more to fight for. At the same time, you will probably feel freer to take more drastic measures than you could before. You've attained a certain level of commitment; you're not desperate, and you're not worried that the relationship will fall apart if you sleep on the sofa to get your point across. Sometimes a woman will be afraid to seem as if she's "making too much" of something; a man may say she's being "petty" or "hysterical." Don't let a man give you grief about this. He's forcing you to scream at him or march off with your pillow to the living room sofa. These are not things you would do if you were dealing with a person as reasonable as you are.

2. He'll overwork.

A man may distance himself from his marriage by working double or triple time. No slouch herself, Dana had her own busy schedule, but she always kept her work hours below fifty. After she and Jim got married, she became what she calls a "work widow." As a consultant with his own business, Jim quickly opened a second office, which required him to spend three days a week in a suburb of the city they lived in. He often worked till midnight no matter where he was. With a schedule such as this, sex became a fond memory—once every few months. (It was good when they had it, Jim insisted during a couples therapy session. "So why not have it more often?" we asked. No one said anything, but the obvious answer was that Jim couldn't schedule it in.) Meanwhile, talking and doing things together had also fallen by the wayside. Before they were married, they'd cook dinner together several nights a week; now, if they met for dinner at all, it was in a restaurant. Their apartment, comfortable and beautifully appointed, was not a home—it was as perfect as a magazine layout and just as unlived-in.

In our first session with the couple, Jim kept an eye on his watch—he had an important business appointment to keep on the other side of the city, and he'd have to jump into a cab the moment our session was over. "This session must be taking valuable time," we said with a straight face. Jim nodded quite seriously—the session was taking time away that could be better spent working, and his anxiety level was hitting the top of the charts. Of course what really made him anxious was that we were talking about his and Dana's feelings; beneath the businessman's exterior was a very different man—one who loved and needed his wife but had no idea how to let her know.

We gave them several assignments right away. First, we would not accommodate Jim's work schedule by meeting with them at midnight, after he was through at the office. He had to come during the day, and he had to keep sessions—no excuses.

Second, there was to be a moratorium on work from Friday night till Sunday night. Third, the couple was to follow at least two of the exercises we described in chapter 7: doing nice things for one another daily, as well as sensual massage so that these two strangers could become reacquainted sexually. And fourth, Jim and Dana were now to eat at home. They must plan meals and cook and eat them together as an exercise in intimacy.

All of this is a tall order for a man like Jim—it'll be a stretch, we told him quite frankly. But he at least understood that Dana meant it when she said she'd leave, and that he had to do something about it if he didn't want her to. He would have to identify the fear that was driving him away from her into a world of obsessive work.

3. He'll be allergic to babies.

Another time when your husband may try to work himself to death will be when you become pregnant. Instead of facing his terror at the idea of having a child (the ultimate commitment), he will go out and get a second job. To you this will feel like abandonment; just when you really need him for support and company, he is remarkable only for his absence. You have to talk to him about this, and set up some of the guidelines we suggested to Dana and Jim. The two of you should understand what his underlying agenda really is. (One important point to remember is that in his own way he may be trying to be nurturing by bringing in more money.) The problem is twofold: first, you need him to be available emotionally, and second, he is missing out on an important experience by not sharing your pregnancy with you.

Once the child is born, your real troubles may begin. Many men feel perfectly justified saying, "Taking care of babies isn't for me. I'm not interested in babies until they reach the age of reason." One sensible, intelligent, otherwise "liberated" man spent an entire session arguing with his wife that women are biologically suited to taking care of babies, whereas men are not. "That's all a justification for not sharing the work with me," she told him. "I wasn't born with a gene for diaper changing."

It *is* an alien experience for a man to take care of an infant. During pregnancy, a woman's body and emotions are reshaped to accommodate another being. And she has learned from our culture that she must give to and nurture other people—she understands that other people can make claims on her. When she has a baby she may find she has no more of a maternal instinct than her husband does, but that she is expected to hustle one up quickly.

In order to keep from ending up in the thankless role of Big Mama, you have to start early with a deliberate program in mind. When you encounter your husband's initial resistance to sharing infant care with you (and no matter how good enough this man is, you *will* encounter it, at least to some degree), do not compensate by becoming more involved with the baby. Before you know it, you will be baby expert and supervisor *extraordinaire;* you will be the one who is in tune with the baby; you'll hear it cry while he "innocently" reads the newspaper. Later, the child will want you whenever she or he needs anything, and you won't have a moment to call your own. Right from the beginning, a man has to have duties to perform.

Divide up the time each of you spends in child care. When it is his turn, leave the house or go into another room and firmly shut the door. Take a hot bath or do something else that is pleasant and relaxing. It is important to let him take care of the child in his own way and make his own mistakes. When one husband was taking care of his infant daughter, he put his foot on her cradle to rock her when she woke up so that he could just finish a few pages of the article he was reading. His wife, in the next room, heard the baby crying and rushed in to scoop her up. This is a mistake! Discuss whether or not to pick up the baby as soon as it cries with your husband—you need to agree. A woman shouldn't look over her husband's shoulder or give him instructions and still expect him to share equally in baby care. In this case, the man *was* taking care of his baby—he needed to be allowed to do it in his own way.

Another woman and her husband decided to take turns getting up at night for feedings. However, once he'd agreed to it, her husband would snore right through the baby's wails. Tuned in to the baby's slightest whimper, she'd lie there nudging her husband and listening to the cacophony of screams and snores for five or ten minutes before her husband woke up. Sometimes she felt sure he was playing a game with her—lying there half awake, hoping she would get up. She finally decided that her choice was to get up and feed the baby herself (out of sheer exasperation) or else insist that her husband do it. She decided to insist. "I punched him until he was black and blue," she says. "And one night I threw cold water on him." Eventually, because she resisted the temptation to let a sleeping dog lie, her husband became more tuned in to the baby's cries and began to take equal share in the night shift.

"I'm afraid that having a baby will change my life." Most people quake at the thought that a little monster is going to open its hungry mouth and swallow up their autonomy. It's true that you give up certain freedoms you may have taken for granted, but sometimes a woman may feel that she has to protect a man from this new reality. She assumes that it is easier for her to give up the freedoms and flexibility in her life than it is for him. She fears that if her husband has to give up any of his autonomy, he will feel tied down. (And then, before she knows it, he'll be saying, "I need my space" or "I feel trapped." Maybe she's heard this from him before.) So, she reasons, if she picks up the slack in child care—if she makes all the sacrifices—then he will be free to lead the same life as before.

Don't protect him. With many men, childcare *can* be a fifty-fifty proposition. We're now seeing men who share both the burdens and the pleasures of child-raising—a radical change from even ten years ago. Even guys who used to stay up all night going to clubs now stay up all night with sick kids. "Sure my life has changed," says one man. "It's gotten better." Many couples rearrange their work schedules so that each works at home a few days a week and takes the lion's share of the baby burden. If you are flexible, you can find solutions. Remember: You don't know what a man is capable of until you both decide that he *is* capable.

4. His affair—her affair.

His. Brad has a fantasy of what it would like to be married. He is a king, who is noble and good. One day he sees her—a beautiful young maiden. Since he is the king, he has all the power, and he can marry her if he chooses. The fantasy has two endings: that Brad and the maiden live happily ever after; or that Brad quickly becomes bored and sends for fresh young virgins to sleep with every night of the week.

Many married men fear giving up the fantasy of the endless sexual smorgasbord; they're sure that sex with the same woman will become an endless yawn. A man may have an affair to per- petuate the fantasy of the omnipresent woman—and to distance himself from his wife.

Jeff had an affair with his tennis partner, then told his wife, Cathy, that he was in love with this woman and intended to marry her. Cathy was stunned; in the five years of their marriage, Jeff had never told her anything was wrong. True, they didn't talk very much, and Jeff had lost interest in her job and friends. This had bothered her, but she hadn't wanted to push him too hard, lest he feel "trapped." But then, a few years later, Cathy says, "He just dropped the bomb in my lap. He didn't feel he owed me anything; he just said, 'I'm not happy, and there isn't anything you can do about it.'" In this case, Jeff's affair was a window out of the commitment he'd made when he married Cathy; the real problem was that he'd never articulated either to himself or to Cathy his problems with intimacy (and Cathy hadn't pushed him to do so).

And what about the other side of the story—the single woman who involves herself with a married man? Know that you are involved with a man who is on the run—in other words even if you tag him, he'll still try to get away.

Judy met Brian at work; during their frequent lunches he told her he was miserable with his wife who was cold, repressed, and asexual. Soon, Judy was in love with Brian, and even though she'd never believed she was the "type" to have an affair with a married man, she soon found herself in a wildly sexual affair with Brian. Nowhere was off limits to them—there was the stairwell at work and the men's room at the end of the hall, where they'd slip into a booth, holding their breath whenever anyone came in (this was part of the thrill; Judy's heart would be beating so hard she'd swear it could be heard). In her apartment they had marathon sex that went on all day and late into the evening, when Brian would finally have to go home.

Judy came to therapy because she was more in love with Brian than ever—and she felt guilty. Was there something wrong with what she was doing? she asked us. The only thing that's wrong, we told her, is that every time Brian has wild, wacky sex with you, you're helping him stabilize his marriage. You're making him a happy man! "He does seem to be talking less about how unhappy he is," Judy admitted. Why shouldn't he be happy? we asked. For great sex he has you; for a dutiful wife, he has *her*.

To a single woman, like Judy, who is involved with married men, we read the riot act—not on moral grounds, but on the grounds that there is nothing in it for her. "What is your fantasy about what's going to happen?" we asked Judy. "That he'll leave his wife," she replied immediately. *"Unlikely,"* we said. "Why should he leave his wife when he has the best of all possible worlds?" And the fact is that even if Brian did leave his wife, he would be a bad bet for Judy. A man who cheats once will do it again. You aren't special to him; you are only one more incarnation of the omnipresent woman of his fantasies.

Hers. Nowadays, a young married woman is just as likely as her husband to have an affair (25 percent of both women and men under the age of 25 have had extramarital sex). And among older women, the figures have risen, too (one study found that 48 percent of married men and 38 percent of married women have had affairs, as opposed to the findings of the Alfred Kinsey survey in the early 1950s that 50 percent of married men but only 26 percent of married women had "cheated"). However, one big difference remains: *For a man, an affair signals a need for distance, while for a woman it is a search for the intimacy missing from her marriage.*

While Pauline sat and took notes in Andre's lecture class, she never dreamed she'd end up his lover, much less his wife. Andre was married and so much more brilliant than she could ever hope to be, she thought. Still, he'd ask her out for coffee after class and always seemed interested in her opinions on everything from literature to politics. Before long, he was asking her questions about her personal life and somehow began telling her about his own pending divorce and how depressing it was to be alone. Pauline felt bad for Andre because the only time he was truly animated was when he was with her; in class and with colleagues he always looked morose. Soon, Pauline and Andre were dating and, a year later, they married.

In their second year of marriage, Andre had an affair—with another student—and confessed to Pauline. She was devastated but decided it was an aberration. She was wrong; when Andre *wasn't* sleeping with someone else, it was an aberration (which was in fact the reason why his first marriage had ended in divorce). In their third year of marriage, Pauline started an affair of her own, with Larry, a faculty member and colleague of Andre's. It wasn't only Andre's infidelity that drove her—it was the painful lack of closeness in the marriage. Any time she wanted to talk, she had to initiate it; it was her total responsibility to keep the temperature of the marriage up (and frankly, she'd cooled off too much to work so hard).

And then came a strange twist: Andre announced that he wanted to have group sex—with Pauline, Larry, and himself as partners! At first she refused, but when Andre pressed her she agreed (she was still a little intimidated by him). So a *ménage à trois* took shape.

Pauline is sure that Andre knows about her affair with Larry, and that he is just waiting for the two of them to betray their secret by showing some special sexual knowledge of one another. But the *ménage* is seductive and titillating, and she continues to participate. By now all three know the marriage is on a collision course and that it is just a matter of time before the impact.

For Andre and Pauline, the problem began with Andre's need for distance, and an ever-widening intimacy gap. And then began the series of affairs that came ever closer to home. Paradoxically, affairs are often an attempt to solve a problem in a marriage. It can function as a way to bring a third party into a difficult situation—and as a way *not* to deal with the disappointments and frustrations within the marriage. But Pauline hadn't really wanted to deal with her problems with Andre; she was readier than she knew to divorce him, and her affair with Larry threw her on an unstoppable trajectory out of her marriage.

Another kind of affair is one that keeps you married but not *well* married. Mary has been having an affair with Tom for the last two years of her four-year marriage to Reggie. For at least three years she has fallen in and out of love with Reggie a million times. He wants to be married but expects her to hold things together: she makes more money than he does; she furnished their apartment (and takes care of it); she is responsible for their social life. If he is in a bad mood, she is expected to take care of him; if she is in a bad mood, well, that's just too bad. Often, Mary longs for her single days, when she was independent and did exactly as she liked. Yet she wants to stay married to Reggie; there is security and familiarity, and even excitement at times, if they haven't seen one another for a while (their work often takes them to two different coasts).

The crazy thing is that ever since she's been seeing Tom, Mary has been much happier with Reggie. She and Tom can really talk, and he can listen to her for hours. She appreciates that. On the other hand, she has no illusions that Tom is the solution to her problems; he is unemployed and usually penniless (his money goes for cocaine). But he does give her some closeness and comfort; he understands her. "I've always had this fantasy of finding a man who really understands me," she says. "I don't believe he exists, but I'm haunted by the idea."

Mary's life is in a delicate balance. Having the affair gives her a sense of autonomy—she has a life outside the marriage—as well as making up for the lack of intimacy within the marriage. By this time she feels that her marriage would not exist without the affair as its secret underpinning.

Our advice to Mary was to turn to the problems in her

marriage and see if they were workable; the affair siphoned her energy away from the problems. She needed to make a decision about her marriage—either she was in or out. She was still straddling the fence, keeping both relationships going.

The new statistics on women and extramarital affairs don't make us applaud. Sure, if men can have sexual adventures, so can women. But the truth is sadder and less simple. While for men, affairs signal a retreat from intimacy, for women, they are symptoms of depression and lack of fulfillment within marriage. Is marriage, as an institution, on the skids?

One woman told us about a small dinner party she'd had the weekend before. Together, she and her husband cooked, and then her husband played with their two year old. All the guests remarked on what a great husband and father he was—he was so involved! "I had a schizophrenic reaction," she says. "On the one hand I was thrilled he was 'helping,' on the other I knew he was doing it for show. After everybody left, I got to clean up and take care of the baby—as usual. And no one's standing there throwing confetti and saying, Wow, what a great mother!" Looking exhausted and depressed, she went on to say, "If I complain about him, I sound ungrateful. I mean, how dare I complain about a guy who's helping so much? Not only that but if I complain, he'll do even less. If I don't complain, I'm accepting the status quo. I'm literally damned if I do and damned if I don't."

Another woman works all day, then comes home and cooks dinner and takes care of her four year old. She literally doesn't sit down until ten, when she collapses in a heap. She hates confrontations, she says, so she avoids demanding that her husband take more responsibility at home. At the same time she feels as if they are becoming strangers. "This is as good as it gets," she says. "I guess he's trying the best he can and I shouldn't get on his back." Meanwhile, her rage turns inward and she is always depressed. Her secret outlet? Movies—alone, whenever she can snatch the time—romantic ones, during which she can have a good cry. And crushes on movie stars—sensitive guys like William Hurt and Harrison Ford who are warm and responsive to women. "It's embarrassing," she says. "I'm an intelligent, adult woman with a good job—and an adolescent fantasy life."

Embarrassing, maybe, but hardly surprising. This woman avoids taking the steps with her husband that she knows are necessary; meanwhile, her frustration and rage fester below the surface, and she cries alone in movie theaters and escapes her reality through fantasy. Other women turn to alcohol and drugs, stay sick, or start shopping or eating binges. It isn't up to you to change a man, but it *is* up to you not to bury your feelings. You must tell him what you need so that he can learn to meet you halfway.

In our practices, we've had good experiences with women who for the first time make demands on their husbands. In a group therapy session, Maya told a story that had the happiest kind of ending. A shy, quiet woman, Maya loves working with children. At the school where she teaches, she and her class decided to put on a play for the whole school and the parents. She and the kids worked for months, and as the big night approached, Maya felt both proud and nervous. She knew that, more than anything, she wanted her husband, Larry, to be there when the curtain rose.

The problem was that she never made demands on Larry. But somehow, she wanted it to be different this time. "It would mean a lot to me if you came to the performance," she told him. Predictably, Larry bitched and moaned. "You're claiming my time," he told her. "I'm too tired to go off and watch a bunch of kids flub their lines." But Maya stuck to it. "I do a lot for you," she told him. "I go to business dinners with you, and we have your colleagues over for dinner. I'd like you to do this for me." Reluctantly, Larry agreed to go.

Larry went—and loved it. The kids were charming and energetic, and Maya's sensitive, humorous touch was wonderfully apparent in the production. She got a standing ovation at the end. Larry was bursting with pride and said to her later, "I never knew this side of your life. It's wonderful." And now, Maya told the group, they were closer than they'd ever been before.

The group applauded Maya, too—for wanting *more* from

her marriage and getting it. But one man, Steven, interjected an altogether different tone. "Be careful of putting demands on men," he said. "It's a big mistake." Everyone looked at him in stunned silence; then they all began speaking at once. "You've given up on your marriage," one woman told him. "You and your wife make no demands on each other," another woman told him. "You're married in name only!"

"Look how empty your life is," another man told him. "You've given up."

Many emotions crossed Steven's face as he listened; at one point we saw tears in his eyes. "It's true," he said. "I *do* feel lonely almost all the time."

That evening, we all shared Maya's elation and Steven's sadness. We all saw the choices that we have. In a marriage or any relationship, you have a right to make demands. If you don't make demands on each other, you're just going through the motions of marriage. Maya understood that sharing her life with Larry had deeper implications for them. That night, for the first time, the two of them became a real couple.

Many men get married but still aren't committed to their partners. A married man is still *really* a bachelor if he:

- Gets home from work earlier than you but still refuses to cook (or even start) dinner.
- Expects you to work a full day at the office and then come home and clean house, pick up his socks, cook.
- Expects you to be the sole nurturer and caretaker of your children; he's there for financial support but not for emotional support.
- Has furtive affairs that you've discovered but which he refuses to discuss with you.
- Works so much that you hardly see one another; his work commitments take place at the expense of *all* your personal time together.
- Refuses to discuss having children.

10

Calling It Quits

Your relationship isn't what you want, or maybe it just isn't going anywhere. You've tried everything, nothing worked, and you know it's finally over. You feel wrung out and depressed—you can't even imagine the day when you'll wake up and feel good (or even human) again. And the sad reality is that this isn't the first or the last time: you'll probably have to manage a number of painful good-byes before you meet a man who can go the whole route with you. Because saying good-bye is so wrenching, many women end up in our offices when they're poised to pull the plug on a relationship. "Am I really doing the right thing?" she—or you—might ask, seeking a shred of hope. And, when you see there is none, you say, "How do I walk away when walking away hurts *this* much?" The problem is that being in the relationship is hurting you even more. Walking away feels like the end of the world *now,* but it is the kind of pain that ultimately cleanses and heals you.

But *why* does it hurt so much to break up? Because, when it comes to relationships, many intelligent, interesting, attractive men turn out to be unable to commit. There's a credibility gap— you literally can't believe that any man who can be so terrific in *every other way* can be so hopeless in *this* way. How can I give him up? you ask yourself. I can't, a voice inside you whispers. Who else is out there? you then ask. No one, you tell yourself. It practically kills you to have to tear yourself away—but you know you're already half dead from the way he's been treating you.

The Good-bye Guy

He doesn't want you to think he's a *bad* guy, or else he's perfectly content with the status quo—this means you will probably be the one who will do the dirty work of ending a bad relationship (even though *he* is the one who forces your hand). Some good-byes are quick; others seem endless. The longer you've been involved, of course, the more tortured the good-bye. There are many different kinds of endings, but they all come as a shock and they all hurt. In this chapter, we'll talk about types of endings that will probably be familiar to you. We think that each of these situations leaves a trail of clues or warning signals—nothing is quite as unpredictable as it seems. We want to emphasize that blaming yourself for missing clues is counterproductive. There are so many men who can't handle relationships that calling it quits is part of the dark side of life for all single woman. You *can* learn to read the signals—as long as you don't waste your time blaming yourself.

What He Does

Suddenly your phone calls are strained, and he seems distant or stilted. "He's acting funny," you note to yourself. "I wonder what's going on." Below is a checklist of some typical kinds of behavior you may pick up on in a man who is leaving without really saying good-bye.

1. He no longer checks in with you regularly by phone.
2. Suddenly his secretary is returning your calls because he "can't get back to you."
3. At home he leaves his answering machine on; you have the sinking feeling he's there, screening his calls.
4. He can't seem to make dates with the same regularity (or enthusiasm) that he used to. Any mention of your usual Saturday night date now makes him squirm.
5. He cuts your dates short or seems just to "fit you into" his schedule at his convenience.
6. He cancels dates, offering excuses such as "I have a cold," or "A friend just dropped into town," or "I have to work."
7. When you're supposed to spend the afternoon together, you find that he's included his best friend in the plans.
8. He snaps at you for "no reason" and does not apologize or explain later that he has problems at work.
9. He criticizes your hair, your friends, your clothes.
10. He no longer wants to spend time with your family and friends.
11. a) He never wants to have sex.
   b) He always wants to have sex.
   c) He accuses you of being sexually demanding.
   d) He accuses you of being sexually boring.
(*Any* change in your sexual pattern that isn't for the better is for the worse.)
12. He is noncommittal about plans you've made together; also, he will not acknowledge the future. If you mention what the two of you might do next summer, his eyes become glassy. Or else he'll change the subject or pretend he hasn't heard you.

What He Says

Good-bye guys are so tricky that we've provided a list of translations to help you read the real message buried beneath the words.

1. "I need my space." Translation: "I have to get out of this relationship."
2. "I don't think you're the one." Translation: "I think there are other women out there who will suit me better than you do."
3. "I'm not ready for a relationship." Translation: "I'm scared that I'm in too deep."
4. "I love you, but I'm not in love with you." Translation: "If you were really right for me, I wouldn't feel so trapped."
5. "I feel trapped." Translation: "I can't go through with this."
6. "Let's be friends." Translation: "I can't be in this relationship anymore, but I hope we can still sleep together when I get horny."

What You Can Do

These translations generally apply to the Good Guy Today/Gone Tomorrow—the man in the middle. A woman intuits something is wrong; let's say the guy is continually muttering about "space" or nothing seems to crack his sexual shell or else he makes and breaks dates like matchsticks. She may think she has to work harder to make the relationship work better. She'll pick up the slack, caulk up the holes with putty, press for more dates and more weekends together. This is the worst thing she can do; a man will recoil as if he's seen a snake. Now is the time to fall back on your grandmother's advice: Don't pursue the guy. Instead— and this *isn't* your grandmother's advice—call him on his behavior. Tell him: "I sense there's something different between us."

With the Good Guy Today, you will probably then have a talk or a series of talks before you can determine if he *is* saying good-bye, or if your relationship needs some fine tuning.

The Long Good-bye

He's just waiting, he might say, for the "right moment" to drop the bad news in a woman's unsuspecting lap (he's really waiting for her to make a move). A man will agonize about how much he doesn't want to hurt a woman—he thinks of himself (and wants you to agree) as a sincere, tortured, angst-ridden guy trying to do the decent thing in letting a woman down easy.

Again, remember that this man, with whom you've probably been involved for at least several months to a year, may be terrific in every other way. He's also demonstrated that he can move at least partially into commitment. Suddenly, though, he feels he has passed the point of no return.

When Gary and Lisa got engaged, they decided that she'd sell her apartment in Atlanta and move to Washington, D.C., to live with him before the wedding. At the same time she arranged for a job transfer. Meanwhile, Gary bought her a ring, and they announced their plans to both of their families. Then Gary went on a sailing holiday for two weeks; when he came back he called Lisa who was still in Atlanta and said, "I feel a little trapped."

"What about our plans?" she asked.

There was a silence, then Gary cleared his throat. "We'd better put them off," he said.

There was Lisa with no apartment and no job in a city hundreds of miles away. Then, a week later, Gary called her and invited her to a special vacation at a Florida spa. "After what you've been through," he said sympathetically, "you deserve it."

Lisa said, "He acted as if 'what I'd been through' had nothing to do with him. He thought we could just jump into a hot tub together after he broke our engagement and completely screwed up my life." She told him to forget the hot tub—and the relationship.

Lisa's experience was not unusual. Unfortunately, a man may take steps along the levels of commitment that he simply isn't ready to take, and then, *bam!* it all hits him right between the eyes. The wedding plans are shot, and so is your life (temporarily). And then, just as typically, the guy will come forth with a friendly offer—how about a terrific, relaxing vacation at a spa? He's trying to "be friends" now; he doesn't want to lose you altogether, and he doesn't want you to think he's a horrible guy.

Never agree to "be friends" with a man who has been your lover immediately after the relationship has ended—this is one of the most deceptively simple yet dangerous plea bargains any man can make with any woman. We recommend that you wait at least six months—or, until you're involved with someone new—before attempting to befriend a former lover.

When Steve began to feel that his relationship with Melissa had gone on too long (they'd been monogamous, at Level Three, for about six months), he told her that he needed space. Melissa correctly translated this riddle as "I want out." Feeling terrible, she took a deep breath and said, "This really hurts me, but I see that you aren't ready to take a leap of faith and go on in the relationship. I guess we shouldn't see each other anymore." Steve agreed.

Then, sometime during the next couple of weeks, he called her and said, "Let's be friends." They resumed the familiar, intimate conversations on the phone that they'd had when they were lovers—only now, instead of making plans to see each other, they'd end the conversations with a feeble, "Well, talk to you sometime." Often Melissa gave Steve advice, and she listened and sympathized with him. Finally, though, she understood that "being friends" was *easing* the break for Steve; if he felt lonely, all he had to do was pick up the phone and call her. And he didn't have to feel guilty, either; since Melissa wasn't mad at him, obviously he wasn't such a bad guy for breaking up with her.

When we asked Melissa why she continued to take these "friendly" calls from Steve, she said she'd thought they might help her through the transitional period after the break-up.

"Is it helping you to let Steve off the hook?" we asked. "Let him confront the consequences of his behavior! These phone calls are interfering with your healing process—every time you hear from him, the wound is re-opened."

The next time Steve called, Melissa told him not to call any more.

And then Melissa got depressed. You may be unpleasantly surprised to find that what is unquestionably a positive move may leave you feeling as if you don't want to get up in the morning.

One antidote is to *allow yourself to get angry.* You've been misled, betrayed, taken down garden paths and dead-end streets. Don't make excuses for him and, above all, resist the temptation to "be his therapist." Before you know it, you'll be helping him ease his guilt about dumping you.

Ask yourself if you're trying to be his friend for any of these reasons:

1. "I'll change his mind." You see the irrationality of his response, and you think you can talk him out of it. You think that with your help, he, too, will see how crazy he's acting. But even if you use all your persuasive powers, you'll never get him back if his heart wasn't in it in the first place.

2. "I'll heal him." By focusing on his feelings, you are trying to avoid your own crushed hopes, anger, and depression. It isn't your job to nurse this man to health; it is your own pain that needs tending.

3. "I'll save the relationship." This is an attempt to apply emergency resuscitation to a relationship that is already dead. You may also feel that where there's talk, there's hope. Unfortunately, in this case you are probably shouting into the wind.

You probably know of long-term relationships that are based on the woman as therapist—but we would never defend any relationship in which a woman accepts the role of caretaker, while a man nestles into the role of helpless infant. Why waste your life?

Get mad instead. Enjoy retaliatory fantasies. Allow yourself the pleasure of raging to your friends about what a complete jerk the guy was.

Many women want a face-to-face showdown at the end of a relationship. *He* has a problem; he's screwed up a good thing, and you want to tell him off. If you do this, fine, but don't get carried away. Plan what you're going to say, rehearse in front of the mirror, or your friends. This is *your* scene, your eloquent soliloquy of rage. Make it plain to him that this is *not* a dialogue and that you will not be drawn into one. Say your piece, and then say good-bye.

What if you make a big mistake? Before you write off a relationship, ask your lover some questions. When Frank told Bette that he didn't think he was "ready" for a relationship, she asked him: "How long have you been feeling this way?" "What was the turning point?" "What exactly would have to happen for you to be ready?" Frank's answers were vague, and Bette was confused. "Call me if you need to talk," Frank urged her at the end of the evening. "How condescending!" Bette thought. "First, he blows me away, then he tells me to call him up and talk, as if I needed his pity." Nonetheless, Frank had left everything so vague that she did call him a few days later. "Are we going to see one another or not?" she asked. Well, he wasn't sure. Call back Wednesday, he advised. "Forget it," Bette told him. "Why should I wait till Wednesday for you to break up with me? I'm breaking up with *you,* right now."

Bette made the right decision. A man's ability to give you specific answers to your questions is critical. If he does, you may find that your relationship simply needs some tuning. When Veronica noticed that Doug was acting "weird," she ignored it at first (hoping it would go away), then asked him if anything was wrong. "Well," Doug said, "now that you mention it, I am concerned about something. Summer's coming, and I really like to play golf all day Saturday at my club, and I don't know how you'll feel about that." It turned out that Doug wouldn't be available to see Veronica until eight P.M. on Saturdays, and he hadn't known how to break it to her. Typically, a man will feel that a woman's *raison d'être* is to erode his playtime; it doesn't occur to him that such things as a relationship and personal freedom can be negotiated.

Veronica asked Doug why he couldn't simply invite her to his club some Saturday so that they could meet for lunch and swimming. Then she said, "Don't you think I have a life of my own? Most Saturdays, I'll be too busy to see you until well into the evening anyway."

In this case, a woman's direct question leads to a needed adjustment in the relationship—not the end of it. If a man is able to continue in a relationship, a question from you should lead to a dialogue. He should be curious to explore what has been bothering him and open to negotiations.

The Short Good-bye

In the case of a Good For Nothing Guy, it usually isn't long before you know you have a choice: wave good-bye to him—or to your sanity. If your sanity wins, you still have to endure a shock to your system. Breaking up with a Good For Nothing Guy *should* be simple; after all, you barely have a relationship. But the feelings you've invested in him, the fantasies and wishes, are powerful—unfortunately, these are *not* so easily broken.

When Rachel met Alan at a party, she sensed before he'd said a word that he'd been through hard times. She was right: he told her that he'd been divorced for a year—and it was clear that he'd not healed from the wound. Since Alan lived in Washington, D.C., and Rachel lived in Philadelphia, it wouldn't be easy for them to see each other again, but Alan said that he planned to visit her on a weekend within the month. Rachel, who had left a three-year relationship a few months before, was delighted. She was cooling out after the stress of the break-up and thinking about what she wanted to do next. She was up for an affair—nothing much, nothing heavy, just some good sex and interesting companionship a couple of times a month. Alan could be the ticket.

Rachel waited for him to call, and when he didn't, she put him out of her mind during the day. She'd recently been promoted to manager at the busy interior design firm where she worked, and she barely had a moment to breathe, much less think about Alan. But her nights were long and quiet, and she'd lie awake wondering why he didn't call. Maybe he just hadn't liked her all that much; maybe there was another woman in Washington. Then one night, he did call, and said he'd like to see her the weekend after next—he'd be coming to Philadelphia on business. Joyfully, Rachel agreed.

Two days before Alan was due to show up on her doorstep, he called and told her he was sick. The weekend was canceled. Rachel tried not to let her voice show how disappointed she really was; nor did she want to admit it to herself. Well, it was hardly the end of the world.

In fact, Alan visited Rachel the following weekend, and the weekend after that. They hit it off beautifully, particularly in bed; she hadn't been that turned on in years! She was used to selfish lovers; Alan, on the other hand, was so sensitive to *her* pleasure that she felt as if they'd been lovers for years. When they weren't together, she wandered through life in an erotic haze, fantasizing and anticipating their next meeting.

Then he broke three weekend dates in a row. Sickness, inconvenience, depression. His life was a mess, he told her. He just couldn't get it together. "Come see me," she urged him over and over again. "Why stay home and be depressed?" When he insisted that he couldn't, she was confused. She knew he was happy with her—his eyes were lively when he was with her and he laughed a lot. So why was he turning down the chance to be happy?

Maybe this was just a passing phase; she'd wait and see. Over the next few weeks, Alan and Rachel spoke on the phone every few days. He was feeling better but not well enough to travel, he said. They discussed his depression, and Alan said he always felt better after he talked with her. Rachel felt more hopeful but decided to say nothing more about visits. If he wanted to see her, he'd make a move. And she felt reasonably sure that he would—the two of them enjoyed one another so much. He'd be crazy to stay away!

Finally, Alan said he wanted to visit her. He was really looking forward to it, he said. Being with her gave him so much energy. . . . For two weeks, Rachel fantasized. "Here I am, thirty-eight years old, and for the first time in my life, all I want to do is have sex!" she told her friends. She went to an expensive lingerie store and bought black silk and lace—quite a change from her usual modest cotton underpants that she jokingly said came up almost to her armpits. She pictured herself dressed in a long, antique silk dressing gown ushering Alan into the softly lit bedroom. By the bed would be an opulent bouquet of peonies perfuming the entire room. He'd slip the gown from her shoulders, and the perfume from her body would envelop them . . . they'd make love all night long.

For two weeks, anticipation built. They called each other and made plans, called each other just to talk. The day before the big weekend, Alan called in the morning, when he knew Rachel would be at work, and left a message on her answering machine. He couldn't make it. No excuses this time. He just couldn't make it. "If you feel like it, call me," he said.

Alternating between despair and rage, Rachel didn't call him. In her heart she knew it was over. Oh, she could keep it going as it was, and maybe once in a while he'd even manage to see her. But he had disappointed her too many times; she'd been running on hope and not much else. Rachel came to understand that while for her an affair was not a commitment; for Alan, it was. For Alan, it was even too much to call her and *tell* her it was too much.

It is extremely difficult to understand this about a man, and it will probably take any woman a few months before she sees the awful truth. There is nothing wrong with you if you don't get it right away, but in the future you can learn to look for clues.

The Relationship That Wouldn't Die

What if you're in a relationship that's on a long, winding road to nowhere? This type is different from the others in that the man won't force you to take a stand. His attitude is "Why break up? *I'm* perfectly happy!" Then, when you finally do break up with him, he hardly seems to care. Remember, though, that men have been trained to amputate their feelings. It doesn't mean your relationship wasn't important to him; it just means that he is numb to his emotions.

As a couple, Jeff was happy and Nancy wasn't. Her idea was

that a relationship has a destination. "It's like a train," she said. "You get on it because it's going to take you somewhere. But for Jeff, it's getting on a train and staying on it till you feel like getting off." It took Nancy two years to realize that she and Jeff were on different tracks.

After Nancy and Jeff had been seeing each other exclusively for a few years in college, they agreed that they'd fallen into the relationship almost too easily. They decided to experiment by seeing other people, by going from Level Three back to Level One. For a few months they dated around, then decided simultaneously there was nothing better out there.

Nancy assumed that once they graduated from college, they'd find an apartment together in the city while Jeff went to business school and she tried to get a job on a newspaper. But to her amazement, Jeff said no; he was tense about school, and he didn't want any complications in his life. He had to get his own apartment. Quickly, Nancy sympathized. "I understand," she said, although secretly she was hurt and confused. Shouldn't he want to live with her as much as she wanted to live with him?

At business school, Jeff became involved in a round of social and professional activities, and even though Nancy was busy with her own job and friends, she always had to accommodate his schedule. "I knew that his work took precedent over me," she said. "He'd spend all day in class or in the library, then he'd meet friends in the evening. If I said anything, he'd act as if I were clinging to him with tentacles. If I didn't say anything, I felt like a doormat." And when she raised the issue of their living together in his second year of business school, Jeff fumbled around for words, then blurted out, "I just can't do it. What if I go out with friends after the library? I'd have to call you."

The whole thing was wrong, Nancy told herself. Maybe she should see other men; maybe her relationship with Jeff would die a natural death. Then she felt terrible. She didn't want to let the relationship die—she still loved Jeff. She'd have to be patient; she'd have to work harder to see that they spent plenty of time together. She turned down dates with other men in order to concentrate all her energy on Jeff. Then came another conflict:

Jeff told her it was too inconvenient for him to come to her apartment on Friday nights, and he wanted her to come to his place instead. Nancy suggested a trade-off; wasn't it fair to take turns? But no, Jeff was adamant; her place was out of his way. Nancy hesitated. She'd been trying to accommodate him in every possible way, but something told her she had to draw the line. "No," she said, "we have to take turns."

Jeff agreed—reluctantly—and Nancy felt hopeful. He *would* come around, if she just kept working at it. But a few days later, she knew it was time to make her plans for the following year; she could spend her whole life patiently waiting for Jeff to make up his mind. She'd speak to him again about living together. "Have a positive attitude," she told herself. "He *will* see it my way."

He didn't. "Living together means we'd end up getting married," Jeff said, actually turning pale at the thought.

Nancy was stunned. "I never said anything about marriage!" she told him. "Forget marriage—I just want us to live together!"

But how could he take that step now? He had loans to pay back, obligations to fulfill. He was too young to be tied down; he had to send money to his parents. This was *awful* for him. Didn't she understand how many responsibilities he had? And another thing had been torturing him, too. How did he know that she was really The One?

"The one *what?*" asked Nancy.

"The one right woman for me," Jeff explained patiently.

"But I thought we'd decided that!"

They stared at each other. Finally, Nancy took a deep breath and said she really wanted them to make plans to live together for the following year. Jeff picked up a day-old newspaper on the table (he'd read anything in order to end a conversation) and from behind it, said, "I can't."

Nancy got up and left without a word. She found her way home, took the phone off the hook, went unsteadily into the bathroom, and threw up.

That night she thought: This relationship is really over. She decided not to see him or speak to him again.

The next day, Jeff called her. "We have to talk," he said. Hope rising, Nancy went off to meet him, imagining him apologizing, telling her he loved her, assuring her they'd be together next year. But Jeff, as it turned out, announced that they couldn't possibly live together for at least two, maybe three more years. Nancy, with an almost giddy sense that she had nothing more to lose, told him he obviously hadn't committed himself to her. "You're right," he said emotionlessly. "I can't commit myself." At that moment the most important thing to Nancy was to maintain her dignity; she would not give him the satisfaction of clawing at him or pleading with him. This was the end—but at least she wouldn't look foolish or pathetic. Dry-eyed, she said good-bye and went home.

A week later, Jeff called her. "Let's have lunch," he said cheerily.

Nancy gritted her teeth. "Don't call me," she said.

"I don't get it," Jeff said. Then, angrily, he added, "You're being irrational."

And that was the end—until the day a few weeks later when they ran into one another on the subway platform (Nancy says now she's sure he planned this "chance" meeting; he never took the subway going in that direction at that time). For the ten minutes until her stop, Nancy listened to her old college sweetheart chat as if they were casual buddies. Those ten minutes were Nancy's longest train ride—and those two years with Jeff were her longest good-bye.

Many men, like Jeff, won't breakup and won't commit. He changes the rules to suit himself, and a woman feels like a rat in a maze. When Bonnie asks Jim when they will get married, he puts her off. "Don't be so impatient," he says. "Just hang in there." She's been hanging in there for four years, and she feels as limp as the Swedish ivy in the living room window. Steve and Jim have all the benefits of intimacy—on their own terms. If a woman wants a relationship on *her* terms, it's *her* move. Often, this will mean the end of the relationship.

We do, however, see more women ending bad relationships

sooner. Break up now: avoid a messy divorce later. It makes sense.

Many women are going into relationships with their eyes wide open; if a man won't pin himself down to make a date for the weekend, a woman is less likely to stay home, dusting her bookshelves and waiting for him to call. If he takes a winter ski house without her and spends a lot of weekends away, she's likely to use that time to see other men and cooly assess one relationship against another.

We would never advise a woman to stay with a man simply because she is afraid to be alone. You need to know that you can live without a relationship. Melissa found that her boyfriend's cold feet were a blessing in disguise—he wasn't right for her anyway. Secretly she'd sometimes been bored with him; he didn't read anything but *TV Guide* and didn't share her love for theater and ballet. "He never stretched himself enough to do new things," she says. "He probably would have ended up being a drag on me, and *I* would have left *him.*"

Ellen discovered that a second-rate relationship is not better than no relationship at all. Ellen is from a traditional, deeply religious family, who had always expected her to marry and have children. When, by the age of 34, she still hadn't, they were almost in despair—if they'd known she was seeing a married man, they might have pretended they didn't know her. But as far as Ellen was concerned, the affair was ideal; she wanted no more commitment from Ian than occasional phone calls and trysts. Then Ian's wife found out about the affair, packed up his things, and threw him out. The next thing Ellen knew, Ian showed up at her door, suitcases in hand. He wanted, he said, to move in with her.

"Oh, no," she thought, "this is *not* what I want." While Ian made himself at home, whistling casually as he hung his suits in her closet, Ellen wrung her hands. She didn't want to hurt his feelings by telling him to go to a motel; nor did she want him horning in on her life. She had some big plans she hadn't told him about yet: she intended to quit her job, buy a camper with her savings, and drive cross-country—alone and free. She wanted to paint and write and explore; she had friends on a Navajo Indian reservation in New Mexico, and she wanted to stay with them for a while. Eventually, she would return to the city, to her apartment, and go back to work.

Now she imagined coming back and finding Ian in her apartment. In the next few weeks, it became clear that he considered himself practically married to her. She admitted to herself that it was pleasant and comfortable to have him around. She *could* marry him; he was beginning divorce proceedings, and he was clearly in love with her. Some of her friends already assumed she would marry him and considered her lucky—there were so few men around, why not grab this guy? As for her family, they were at first aghast when a male voice answered her phone, but soon began hinting about the wedding. As for Ian, he dismissed her plans to travel as if they were a childish daydream, and whenever she expressed doubts about their future together, he told her she had a problem with commitment. Well, maybe she did; maybe she should just drop her plans and let the inevitable happen. . . .

It wasn't easy for Ellen to bear Ian's anger or her family's disapproval, but she had a stubborn, independent streak that helped her stick to her plans. She bought the camper and set a date for departure. She told Ian she wasn't ready to live with him or marry him, and that she didn't know if she ever would be. He could stay at her place while he looked for his own apartment, but it was strictly temporary. When she came back from her travels, they would see where they stood with one another.

We've often seen men—the great space-shielders!—move in on a woman without once considering *her* space. Ian simply assumed that Ellen would want to marry him and accused her of having a commitment problem when she didn't want to. Can women have cold feet? Some women shy away from commitment or end relationships because they've been burned in the past, but in Ellen's case this is sheer nonsense. The time and the man were not right for her; a second-rate relationship (ending in a second-rate marriage) based on self-sacrifice would have killed her spirit.

When you're trying to determine whether or not a relationship is worth continuing, here are some questions, and typical answers the three types of guys will respond with, that will help you determine whether or not the relationship is going to work:

Question 1: I sense there's something different between us—Do you feel the same way?

GOOD ENOUGH GUY	GOOD GUY TODAY/ GONE TOMORROW	GOOD FOR NOTHING GUY
Yes, let's talk about this! Since we've been seeing each other I feel cut off from my friends.	We're seeing too much of each other. I think we should cool it.	There you go again—you make a big deal out of everything.
Translation: I want to work toward a solution so that I can be with you and my friends as well.	I'm panicked.	I don't want to listen to you—you're too much trouble.
Advice: Work out a specific schedule.	Try to negotiate a relationship at a lower level of commitment in which he will feel safer.	Don't blame yourself; move on if what you want is a relationship.

Question 2: How long have you been feeling this way?

GOOD ENOUGH GUY	GOOD GUY TODAY/ GONE TOMORROW	GOOD FOR NOTHING GUY
Since we made plans to take a vacation together.	I really can't say. I guess always.	What way?
Translation: I've never spent two weeks alone with a woman I care about and I'm scared.	Closeness suffocates me.	Women! I don't know what you're talking about.
Advice: Discuss whether the vacation together is premature; be prepared to cancel plans and take a weekend away together instead.	Reassure him that you like privacy, too, and don't want to rush things.	It's obvious that you should leave this guy, if you haven't already.

Question 3: I wish you would have said something sooner—what prevented you?

GOOD ENOUGH GUY	GOOD GUY TODAY/ GONE TOMORROW	GOOD FOR NOTHING GUY
I thought about it, but I was waiting for the right moment	I don't know. What's the big deal?	(Shrugs his shoulders and looks away)
Translation: I wanted to talk about it but I was scared to bring it up.	If I ignore this it will go away and she will forget about it.	Don't bother me.
Advice: Reassure him that you want to talk about his feelings.	Let him know it's a bigger deal if you *don't* talk about it.	You shouldn't even be talking to the Good For Nothing Guy. He doesn't take you seriously enough.

Question 4: What would you like to change between us?

GOOD ENOUGH GUY	GOOD GUY TODAY/ GONE TOMORROW	GOOD FOR NOTHING GUY
I wish we could talk more. I really feel better when we discuss these things.	I need more time for myself. How about if we see each other only on weekends?	Let's just hang loose.

Translation:

Talking is difficult for me, but I think it's important.	I'm not ready for an intense relationship.	Don't count on me for anything.

Advice:

Be encouraging even when he says things that are hard for you to hear.	Listen to what he says; Don't delude yourself that you are further than Level Two, steady dating; see if a more casual relationship works for you.	Move on from this guy; he's not capable of maintaining a relationship.

NOTE

The next chapter is just what it says—For Men Only. (You'll probably want to read it, too, but it's perforated so that you can tear it out and give it to the man you're involved with.) Ask him to read it, then tell him you'd like to discuss it with him afterward. It won't take much time—maybe ten minutes. This chapter will probably be the first of its kind that he's ever read, so be prepared for some pretty strong reactions!

11

For Men Only

Your girlfriend or wife has just dropped this book into your hands, open to this page. "Oh, no," you groan. You hate to read advice books. You're sick of the word "relationship," and you don't want to be lectured about "sharing" and "caring"; you suspect it's all a conspiracy to get you to give up your freedom and independence—your *life*. And anyway, you *do* try to work out your problems with women—you're a good guy, basically, so what now? Why should you read this chapter in this particular book?

Maybe because something still seems a little off in your relationships with women. Here you are, functioning like a star in every other aspect of your life, yet somehow you can't make a go of it with any one woman. It may seem to you, for example, that she's always on a tear about something—why are the two of you constantly chewing over "the relationship" instead of having fun? Or maybe you've just broken up with a woman because she hassled you and you didn't have enough space, but now you're knocking around your apartment feeling on the outs. We had a client named Nick, for example, who broke up with with his girlfriend, Monica, because she was always "bugging" him about something. Yet now he finds he misses her; all of his friends are getting married, and he's alone.

If this guy could be your brother, your best friend, or you, you'll be glad to hear that we have some ideas that might help. Our research has shown that, these days, relationships between men and women are out of whack, and that men have to work to make the pieces fit. Women are demanding more from relationships, and men are afraid to give more and get closer. Women want to know *today* where a relationship is going tomorrow. There's good news and bad news. The good news is that you've got a terrific woman—she's dynamic, challenging, sexy, and assertive. The bad news is that *you* have to change.

Try this short test:

Do you feel or assume that the woman in your life

1. is too demanding?
2. pries into your affairs?
3. invades your "space"?
4. never wants you to spend time with your friends or have any activities of your own?
5. Do you think that having a relationship means smothering your freedom and autonomy?

If this sounds pretty familiar to you, we think you are reading this woman wrong.

You were brought up to believe that women are space invaders and that you have to defend yourself against them. We'd go so far as to say that in another era, you might have been right. But today's woman doesn't *want* your independence, your time, your space, your freedom, your money, or your soul. *She wants her own independence, her own time and space . . .* everything that *you* want. Excessive closeness is probably just as repugnant to her as it is to you; the point in *any* relationship is to find a good balance between independence and intimacy. You may agree with this in principle, but, in fact, even the word *intimacy* makes you break out in a chill. The problem is that you, like other men, have cold feet.

When we told colleagues that our book had a chapter for men only, they said, confidently, "Forget it. Men wouldn't be caught dead reading anything that tells them they have to change." Why should you take this kind of bad press lying down? Prove them wrong and read on.

Three Men

We're going to describe three different situations that spell relationship trouble. You will probably be able to relate to at least one of them. Will we then prove to you that it's all your fault and condemn you to fifty lashes at dawn? No, not exactly, but beware: we *are* talking about taking responsibility.

"She isn't the right one."

You have serial relationships with terrific women. One by one, these relationships go belly up as soon as it becomes clear that the woman is not perfect. You tend to find fault with women, and often you end up hating those very qualities that first attracted you to her. Because no woman is perfect, you run through relationships as if they were Kleenex. If you don't realize what you're doing, at some point you'll have gone through the entire population of desirable, eligible women; *and then what?*

There is no perfect woman, as you probably realize when you're being rational. You also know that life is filled with problems that need solving—you do it on the job; you just aren't willing to do it with women. In fact, as soon as you sniff a problem in the wind, you bolt. At the beginning of the relationship, all is passion—a real rush! But as soon as you get to know her and she makes more demands on you, the spell is broken.

There are three stages in the natural course of any love relationship: the first is idealization (she's your dream woman); the second is disillusionment (she's all too real); and the third is resolution (she's human, but you love her in spite of it). This is the way we *all* fall in love, out of love, and back in love again. The harder you fall, the more disappointed you may be, so you shouldn't be surprised by the emotional roller coaster. Remember: If you didn't idealize, you would never fall in love. No one wants to miss out on that overwhelming, giddy experience in which the whole world is transformed and filled with novelty and beauty. But part of the beauty of it is that it's *brief*—it *isn't* everyday life, it's special. Take it for what it is and move on from there.

Your problem is that you don't move on. You quit just when it's time to get started. But phase three—resolution—is critical. This is when a relationship deepens—when you aren't dealing with a woman as you want her to be, but as she really is. If you get this far, your earlier romantic feelings may be reborn—many people are amazed to find that when they know one another intimately, the romance is even richer.

Don't run—stick it out!

Okay, you say, but what if the relationship really is wrong? What if she is *not* the right one? This is a perfectly legitimate concern—the answer is that if it is wrong, you will know it. But first, you have to wait around long enough to be sure. Maybe she isn't right for you—but why set yourself up to be disappointed before you give it a chance?

There are two telltale variations of the serial pattern. First is the long-distance relationship; if you're bicoastal, for example, you can idealize with only those few rude interruptions when you actually see each other. Second, the on again/off again relationship, in which constant crisis acts as a prophylactic against intimacy—you don't trust there can be real, lasting excitement between you, so you're always breaking up and making up. The point with both of these situations is you don't trust that you can feel turned on by a woman you know and who knows you. The point, again, is to find out with a real person.

Recently we've noted a puzzling phenomenon that may be familiar to you in which a man with a history of serial relationships abruptly marries a woman he barely knows.

An ex-client scheduled an appointment to see us; he wanted

to tell us he was getting married in June to a woman he'd met in December, and that there was going to be a huge wedding with all the trimmings, and that he was the happiest man on earth. We waited for the other shoe to drop; no one comes to therapy to marvel at a state of bliss. When he said nothing further, we said, "Is there a problem, Rich?" He looked at us in surprise. "Why, no," he replied. "Well," we said, "it isn't that we aren't delighted to hear that you're happy, but somehow it seems as if something must be wrong. Why else would you be here? Couldn't you have just dropped us a note about the wedding?"

Rich got angry. "Why are you so cynical?" he asked. *"Nothing* is wrong."

In July, Rich and his bride, on the verge of divorce, were in our office. *Everything* was wrong.

Had they foreseen any problems before the marriage? Yes. In fact, they'd decided there were so many problems that they'd better get married pronto—or else they'd never get married at all. We mentally groaned. Marrying *instead of* facing your problems or dealing with normal disillusionment is like closing your eyes and making a wish. Don't think you can "keep it light," get married, and *stay* married. Before you know it, serial relationships will turn into serial marriages—and that is painful.

We tell our male clients to approach a relationship the way they approach a job: knowing there will be problems, but confident of their ability to solve them. You know from your work experience that when you take on a problem, you have more control; you can use your wits, flexibility, and imagination to figure out thorny issues. You don't feel hopeless about problems in other aspects of your life, so why should you feel that way about relationship problems?

Speaking of work, try thinking of an emotional partnership this way: in business, two partners agree to share expertise and resources, to benefit from one another's differences, and to profit as a team. In a relationship, two very different people agree to work out their differences for their mutual good. In both cases, navigating may be tricky, but the benefits may far exceed your initial outlay.

"I Can't Jump the Hurdle"

You're 27, and you've been living with Janis for a year. She's talking about your future together, but you can't see it. You feel you've given the relationship a chance, but that Janis just isn't the right woman for you. You also feel that you're just not ready to commit to *any* woman and settle down for good. The fact is, you're tired of women seeing you as a "marriage object."

Fine—don't pressure yourself to do something you don't want to do. Women feel the urge to nest earlier than men do, and that's why she's pushing you further than you want to go. Keep in mind that the biological clock is a fact of life for a woman, and that she *has* to think in terms of it. We understand that this could be offensive to you, but we'd also be very surprised if most women you meet actually see you *only* as marriage fodder. Your response —not wanting to commit to this woman at this time—is perfectly normal, valid, and justifiable for a man in his mid- to late twenties.

Now, we'll change the scenario in a key way. Let's say you're 34 and have been involved with Joyce for three years. She is talking about your "future" together for the first time, and has mentioned more than once the terrible clock as well as the dreaded "M-word." When you don't want to talk about it, she gets upset. Now she's told you that if you don't see a couples therapist with her, she's going to donate all the clothes you've left at her place to the Salvation Army and start seeing other men. You certainly don't want her to do *that;* on the other hand, you don't want to sign on the dotted line. The two of you have too many "problems." What should you do?

Check out the "problems." There may be specific areas to be worked out; on the other hand, your cold feet may have turned into blocks of ice at the very notion of deepening intimacy. So, go to therapy and find out where the trouble lies. Be prepared to learn that you may have a vested interest in *not solving* some of the problems you uncover. On the other hand, you care deeply about Joyce, and you don't want to lose her.

What will therapy be like? Hard—but challenging. Maybe you'll bring up all the problems the two of you have, which to your way of thinking make it impossible to talk about a future together. When you do talk about the problems, Joyce will be surprised. "Why didn't you tell me about all this before?" she'll ask. "Because I never thought of this relationship as permanent," you protest, "so why bother? And not only that," you add, "now we're in a relationship that has problems . . . before, we could just have *fun*."

It's catch-22 time for Joyce. As long as she keeps quiet about the future, everything is fine between the both of you. The moment she demands to know what to expect from you, you throw a roadblock in her path—problems she never knew existed. But the fact is you may be finding fault with Joyce in order to protect yourself. You may also find that the more Joyce talks about the future, the more "imperfect" she becomes. Many of the problems you raise are probably fairly minor and, most important, manageable. We're not saying this woman doesn't have her faults, but if you truly do love one another it's possible to handle even fairly heavy problems without giving up.

It isn't that you want to jettison the relationship—you just want to keep it status quo. In the heat of the moment she accuses you of letting things go stale—you just as hotly deny it. You want to live for the *moment,* you tell her. And you *believe* this; on the other hand, you have the sneaking feeling she may be on to you.

To be honest, thinking of the future scares you; it's safer to push the hold button. You may, for example, have noticed that while sex was great at the beginning of your relationship, it's blah now. Well, you don't really care, you say; after all, you're both very busy. Come on—do you really buy this, or is it a rationalization? You suspect the latter: if you expect more from sex, it'll just get you in deeper, so you do without good sex to avoid having to give more to Joyce. But we're sure you'll agree that as a young, vital guy, you should be having great sex—and you can, once you resolve your fear of intimacy.

And that's what's going on here: fear. *Yours.* When you are 26 or 27, you're skimming the edges of relationships; you aren't ready for the depths. By the age of 34, however, if you are in an intimate relationship with a woman whom you love, it is not

[197   ]

premature to talk with her about the future. Take steps to do so before *she* takes steps . . . right out of your life.

"Why Doesn't She Get Off My Case?"

You're in a relationship with (or maybe married to) Linda. Everything would be fine if she'd just lay off. Bitch, bitch, bitch. This woman never lets up: if it isn't the housework you don't get around to doing, it's complaints about your not spending enough time talking with her and doing things with her. According to her, you're also a miser when it comes to sexual foreplay. Well, nagging and complaining are hardly aphrodisiacs.

We agree. We'd hate the feeling that someone was always clobbering us over the head. You constantly feel as if she wants more from you than you want to give. "I'm a stone," you want to tell her. "Stop trying to get blood!" You wish you could wear a sign that says in capital letters: LEAVE ME ALONE! If only she were happy, then you'd be happy, too. "What's the problem?" you're always asking. "Everything seems fine to me." Basically, you just want her not to want anything.

This is a serious problem. What should you do? First, understand that *you* have reduced her to this sorry state! She's nagging because she can't get through to you. You want things strictly on your terms; you love being taken care of, but you don't want any hassles and you don't want to put any sweat into maintaining the relationship. When you get right down to it, you are a guy that isn't crazy about giving. (Join the crowd: this is one of the most common experiences men have in relationships with women.)

You are being barraged because you want to be detached and she wants to be involved. Take it as a compliment that she wants more of you, not less. And you *will* have to change in some ways. Every week, you should set aside time to talk openly with her about your feelings or something you feel vulnerable about. You may not feel at first as if you are giving freely to her or benefiting from the experience, but, after a while you will feel so enriched, so much more self-aware that you will wonder what all the fuss was about.

We suggest that you take frequent responsibility for creating intimate moments between the two of you. Plan a dinner at a romantic restaurant you've heard of. Plan outings the two of you would enjoy, or maybe something on the spur of the moment, such as a play, or a movie on a weeknight. Or, act on an impulse. One couple, harried, hot, and hostile to one another during a shopping trip for a sofa bed, had an intimate moment in the basement of a discount furniture store. While the Muzak mangled a Frank Sinatra tune, the man grasped his girlfriend around the waist and waltzed her down the aisle. Everyone else thought they were crazy, but so what? This couple felt closer and more in love in that tacky basement, on that terrible day, than they had in months.

Anytime you're the one to initiate intimacy, you'll feel less leery of it. Also, be sure to bring up the issues that bother *you*—- why should she be the only one to muckrake the relationship? Choosing intimacy will be going against the grain for you, but look at it this way: maybe, perversely, you *like* the fact that she's always trying to pound down your door. You feel pursued and not a little superior—you have something she wants.

Nowadays, women are very self-aware: they know what they want and they know when they aren't getting it. And, when a woman can't get what she wants, she'll take her business else-where. She'll give up on a man who can't give, and find a man who can. How can you prevent this? It's simple—meet her half-way.

Odd Man Out

You're the guy who's always on the lam, has no relationships and is basically a curse on women. At first we thought, why bother talking to you in these pages? You'll never listen.

But that didn't seem quite right. There's a lot of you guys out there, and you can be pretty charming, and we're prepared to defend your right to be just as charmingly uncommitted and utterly hopeless as you are. Basically, we want to say one thing: Be up front with women. The biggest distinction lies between those of you who are and those who aren't. If you tell a woman right away, flat out, that you aren't interested in a relationship, you're giving her a fair shake. If she insists on trying to reform you, that's her lunacy. If, however, you play along with her and misrepresent yourself, *that* is downright sleazy.

And not only sleazy but unnecessary. One man we know who is notorious for his pursuit and conquest of women, says: "Why should I lie? I have affairs with plenty of women just by being straight with them about who I am and what I want. It's much better that way—no complications."

But if you're a guy who *does* want relationships, expect complications. They're normal. We insist to women that they take not more than 50 percent of the responsibility for a relationship; at the same time we tell men to take *at least* 50 percent. "You mean I should take *more* responsibility than she does?" you ask, aghast. Well . . . you may have to give until it hurts, at least for a while, as you try to get things into synch. At this point women have given too much, and you have given too little. Your goal is to create a genuine give-and-take, a fine balancing act that is the secret of every successful relationship.

Your Commitment Profile: Are You Ready for a Commitment?

This is a test to help you identify areas of difficulty in your relationships with women. Check your score against ours. Your Commitment Profile will tell you how ready you are for a committed relationship.

Rate each statement on the questionnaire according to the following key:

Never	Rarely	Sometimes	Often	Generally	Always
0	1	2	3	4	5

I feel . . .

1. she wants me to do things her way.
2. she is pushing me into living together.
3. she always wants to talk about "The Relationship."
4. she is critical.
5. she is demanding.
6. I'm always making concessions.
7. her family is *her* problem.

I feel it's perfectly reasonable . . .

8. to wait until the last minute to make our dates.
9. not to have to account for my time when I'm alone.
10. to keep all my options open.
11. for her to make all our social plans.
12. to keep my friends and business associates separate.
13. to expect that my life shouldn't change because I'm in a relationship.
14. to feel annoyed when she asks me to help her with her career.

15. to come on stronger that I really feel so that I won't hurt a woman's feelings.

16. to wait a few days after we have our first sexual experience to call a woman again.

17. to spend a portion of every weekend alone.

18. to have sex and then ask a woman to leave.

19. to tell a woman I'll call her when I have no intention to in order to let her down easy.

20. to ask her to split the bill on the first date.

21. to send her home on her own because I have a busy day tomorrow.

22. to squeeze her in at the end of the evening if I'm having a very busy week—it's better than nothing at all.

23. to ignore her when she's pushy—after all, who needs a fight.

During lovemaking, when she tells me what turns her on, I think . . .

24. she's too aggressive.

25. what a turn on!

26. I thought we settled that already.

27. why is she asking, she knows I hate doing that.

28. it breaks the mood.

29. I'm uncomfortable.

30. why didn't she wait to tell me afterward?

31. she's always telling me what to do.

When I want to have sex and she's not interested . . .

32. I masturbate.

33. I sulk until she gets the message.

34. I think this is a very big problem.

35. I try to seduce her and turn her on.

36. she should realize that I need sex to relax.

37. I think about other women.

38. I think the next time she wants sex and I don't, I'll remind her how it feels.

39. I think her sex drive is not strong enough.

When she wants to have sex, and I don't . . .

40. I go through the motions, but my heart isn't in it.
41. I wish she'd lay off until this project I'm working on is completed.
42. I feel pressured.
43. I'm tired of her demands.
44. I feel obligated to accommodate her.
45. I won't cuddle with her because I don't want to lead her on.
46. I don't even want to be touched.

I feel intruded upon . . .

47. when she wants me to spend Thanksgiving at her parents' house.
48. when I'm expected to help in the kitchen.
49. when I'm expected to know what she wants.
50. when I have to call home to tell her I'll be late for dinner.
51. in general.
52. when she books up our weekend.

I wish that . . .

53. we'd never fight.
54. she'd get off my back.
55. she'd loosen up.
56. give me more time to decide about the relationship.
57. I'd never said "I love you."
58. we could turn the clock back to when we first met.
59. she would be more feminine.
60. I could really be sure that she's the right one.

It drives me crazy when . . .

61. she makes any decision that affects me.
62. she talks about her "biological clock."
63. she wants me to express my feelings more.
64. I never have enough time for myself.
65. she won't come to my place all the time.
66. her feminist friends come over.

Scoring Your Commitment Profile

Under 75: You're too good to be true! You're not being honest with yourself. You tend to deny your feelings until it's too late.

75–150: You are probably already in a committed relationship. You are honest enough to admit that some things bother you, but commitment is not a problem. Intimacy comes easily to you.

150–200: The commitment barrier is not going to overwhelm you. You have good relationships but are sensitive to loss of freedom when you get close to a woman. Although you have to work actively at keeping communication open, closeness does not scare you off.

200–250: You are ambivalent about closeness with a woman. You want to commit, but you have to struggle to sustain your relationship. Take stock of your pattern in a relationship and try to catch yourself blowing hot and cold.

250–300: You have a serious problem with intimacy and push the panic button early on in a relationship. You are likely to hurt the women you love because you view relationships as a major threat to your autonomy and independence.

300 and over: Your cold feet require thermal socks. You are not even trying to relate, let alone to commit. Be honest—tell her you are not interested in a relationship.

Isn't That the Way
Love Should Be?

Don is in love with Julia and committed to her, but as Julia says, "Sometimes you wouldn't know it." He isn't as attentive to her as she is to him; he never lets her know when he's going to be late, for example, and tends to feel crowded when they spend a lot of time together. "Why do I always have to check in with you?" he asks irritably. "Why do I have to be accountable to you for my time?"

"If you really love somebody," Julia says, "you just *do* those kinds of things. Isn't that what love is all about?"

The answer to Julia's question is: ideally, yes, but realistically, no. We told Julia that she really can't expect Don, or any man today, to be automatically responsive and attentive. To put it bluntly, men just aren't *there* yet. Meanwhile, *you* have to take the initiative and make demands on him so that he can learn how to be intimate with you. Eventually, if enough women do this, cold feet will become yesterday's fashion.

We wrote this book because relationships between women

and men are changing—fast. Nowadays, the *only* reason for a man and woman to get together is for emotional intimacy— women's financial dependence and men's emotional dependence have gone the way of the Edsel. *For the first time ever, women and men have to meet one another halfway.*

Because intimacy is the keystone, the issue of men's cold feet has come into direct focus. Our task now, in the 1980s and 1990s, is to overcome men's problems with intimacy. Today women have expectations they never had before; they want more—and are *demanding* more—from men. The idea of "making demands" has been misconstrued and badly maligned—now, making demands means giving voice to the deepest expectations a couple may have of one another. Making demands means that a woman such as Julia takes the first step toward making a new kind of relationship.

"What do you demand of each other?"

The couple looked blankly at us, then at one another. The question clearly made them uneasy, and they didn't know how to respond.

Exercise 8.   We've saved this one till last, because in some ways it has become the most important intimacy exercise for today's couples. If you can't make demands on one another, you aren't in a relationship—and for many couples this comes as news.

The long-term relationships we see in our offices usually fit into one of three categories: in the first, the man backslides and the woman picks up the emotional slack; in the second, both the man and the woman have given up on intimacy altogether; and finally, in the third, both the man and the woman work hard at intimacy. *Only* in the third category do women and men make mutual demands on one another.

Intimacy has always been defined in terms of two people exposing their needs, raw nerves, and soft spots to each other. The next step, making demands, is much harder—and most people don't want to hear about it. In the first category of long-term relationship, the woman's role has been a shoulder-to-lean-on;

the man has assumed his needs will be met—quietly, efficiently, and without any fuss and bother. For a woman, exercise 8 may be the hardest one of all. A woman who is used to responding to a man's demands must learn to feel entitled to tell him, "This is what *I* need from *you.*" For his part, he must respect her needs and take them seriously.

Recently, Anna began making demands on Phil. Each of them works part-time at home, and Anna usually found herself immersed in Phil's emotional and professional needs instead of her own. If he happened to be "blocked" (he's a commercial artist), he'd walk in and out of her office and complain about how difficult his work was. To put exercise 8 into effect, Anna has set up what she calls "office hours"—from seven in the morning until two P.M.—during which she cannot be disturbed. "I need my space!" she said, teasing Phil with the same words he'd used in the past when her need for closeness made him uncomfortable. Anna still needs closeness, but now, as a graduate student writing her dissertation, she also requires long hours to think and write and do research. She realized that she spent so much time on Phil's work and Phil's problems that it would be at least another five years before she'd get her Ph.D. (four years had already somehow slipped by since she'd started).

Anna's demand shook their relationship to its very roots. Now that she has told Phil that she wants him to respect her time and space, he has to make *specific* demands on her, whereas before he simply expected her to fulfill *all* his needs, *all* the time. (And, automatically, she did.) His demands now are that Anna spend time listening to and talking with him (the same demands she used to make on him!). Now that women are focusing more on their own needs, men are being forced to spell out what they want. It is up to *both* of them to be in charge of their life as a couple, and up to each of them to find a comfortable balance between personal space and closeness. "We have to renegotiate our relationship," Anna told Phil thoughtfully in a session. "I love you and I want this relationship, but things are going to be different now."

Phil's initial reaction was to sulk; he *hates* the very idea of

Anna withdrawing any part of herself from him. Anna's initial reaction was to feel guilty. At this point we jumped in. "Don't give guilt a chance," we said. "Phil was more comfortable with some of the old ways, and he'd like you to go back to them. Resist this." To Phil, we said, "This will take some adjusting for you. But we guarantee that the reward will be worth the pain."

One Demand a Day

For many women, making demands makes anxiety. Even for a woman like Anna, who is competent, poised, and self-sufficient in her professional life, it's tough. *Demand* is an ugly word; being a demanding woman is tantamount to inclusion in the great sisterhood of "bitches" we talked about in an earlier chapter. A man's difficulties with making demands are different: most men feel *too* entitled to make them. *"Of course she should give me what I want and need!"* However, when a man has to make his demands *explicit,* he may start stuttering. An embarrassment factor comes into play when he has to acknowledge that he has needs. As long as a woman automatically fulfills them, he doesn't have to admit how much he relies on her.

Because making one demand a day is so difficult for women and men alike, we tell couples to think of three things they'd like their partner to do for them. A few suggestions are: Would you like your partner to wait up for you if you're late coming home from the office? Would you like to have dinner together twice a week or to spend weekends together instead of working? Would you like him or her to prepare dinner for you on occasion? These demands are most helpful for the second category of couples: those who seem to have given up on intimacy as a bad bet, then find themselves feeling lonely and depressed.

A Modern Horror Story

A while ago, a magazine article devoted to the new modern couple presented what is actually a modern nightmare: couples on the fast track, each with a high-powered career, catching each other at ten at night or colliding accidentally in the bathroom, living together like roommates or two uninhabited business suits. For all the contact they have with one another, you could just as well arrange two resumés side by side in bed, tuck them in, and call *that* a relationship.

It was as if a man with a bad case of cold feet had sketched out a blueprint for his ideal relationship—no intimacy, total autonomy, with enough space between two people to drive a Mack truck through. Now that the nurturing female has flown the hearth, no one tends the home fires—but are two "husbands" living together an answer to the problem of who *should* tend it? Obviously not. The businessman's model for a relationship seems to make intimacy a quaint relic of the past, but in the long run it will never work. Couples on the fast track can be derailed: what if, suddenly, one loses a job or gets sick and is no longer completely autonomous? What if one wakes up in the middle of the night and, in the stillness after the frenetic pace of the day, feels suddenly lonely and empty? This could happen someday, and at that point, at least one of you will realize that you need the other.

Even if you aren't in this extreme form of the autonomous relationship, it may strike you that you and your partner haven't spent time together in weeks, not even just to sit and talk. In this case, the two of you have to work harder at intimacy. The more separate and busy your lives are, the more important it is that you make your one demand a day. Super-autonomous men and women may be equally afraid to do this—closeness and reciprocity result from making demands of one another. Suddenly, you realize that your lives are interrelated, that you need and depend on one another. A self-sufficient woman who has worked hard to achieve her autonomy may fear being sucked into a more traditional role; she doesn't want to admit *any* craving for closeness because, to her, closeness spells *dependency*. She also knows from experience that if she begins to pick up the emotional slack in a relationship, it quickly becomes *her job* to do so.

For the autonomous couple, we suggest that if both work late, the first one home should make dinner for both (instead of each grabbing a sandwich at the deli). If a woman doesn't want to cook (and many women don't, for fear of becoming permanent kitchen help), she can legitimately demand that her partner take most of that responsibility while she takes on the greater part of the shopping or cleaning up.

We also suggest that couples have check-in times with one another; if your partner is expecting you at 7:30 and you realize you'll be home closer to 9:30, phone home. With Alexis and Peter, time was at a premium, so as part of their therapy we suggested they meet for dinner a few times a week. The problem was that when Peter was going to be late, he didn't call. This demand made him itch—why should he be accountable to Alexis for his time? But calling home is simple and straightforward: "You should be flattered that someone wants to see you," we said. "Alexis isn't trying to nail you to the wall, she just likes to be with you."

One couple we know, who have very separate and autonomous lives, are in a cliffhanger situation: the man flirts with other women and stops just short of having affairs. He won't stop short forever; what he hasn't articulated to himself or his wife is a need for closeness with her. She may have the same need, but neither has demanded it of the other. *Particularly* if the two of you are very autonomous, you must declare openly and without hedging the sexual inviolability of your relationship. You must be fully able to trust and depend on your partner, and vice versa. If not, the relationship won't play.

The New Relationship

We're prejudiced; we admit it. We believe that the third category of relationship, in which couples work at intimacy, is the *only* kind really worth having. If, for example, Anna sticks to her guns about focusing on her own needs and demanding that Phil respect her time and space, then there will be *two* creative, productive people in the family, instead of just one. With each person aware of the other's needs, Anna and Phil are more than just two individuals randomly hooked up to one another—surrounding them is a closely woven web of support that provides help, security, comfort, and love.

We'll make a prediction. As the men and women of this generation change, they are laying the groundwork for big changes in the generation to come. Alice, a teenager, announced to us that she has a new boyfriend. "Is he a good boyfriend?" we asked. She knew immediately what we meant. "Yes," she said. "He pays attention to little things, like waiting for me after class. He always makes plans in advance, and he doesn't mind if I call him. I don't have to sit around waiting for *him* to call. We're friends."

Alice's question isn't: "Does he like me?" Instead, it's: "Do I like *him*?" In the way that we suggested in the first chapter, Alice takes a cool view of men and sees them objectively; she stands back and evaluates them. Her criteria aren't whether or not he's popular or the captain of the football team, but whether he behaves toward her in a way she likes.

In the past, women hoped that men would like them and blamed themselves if they didn't. They groped around in the dark, trying to figure out how to judge men and evaluate relationships. In this book, we've emphasized gaining analytic tools, such as an understanding of the three types of men, and the Five Levels of Commitment. Changing your relationships is difficult: you must first acknowledge your fear and anger, then you must speak up for yourself. Finally, you learn how to make demands.

He may call you a nag or a bitch; you may think you'll lose him or that he'll never change. But once you know what your needs are, you have a fighting chance of having them met. At that point neither of you can stay the same, nor can you go back. For you, the reward for knowing and stating your needs may very well be a more egalitarian relationship. For him, the reward for overcoming his cold feet is learning how to be more intimate.

Even Superman has changed. The *New York Times* recently reported that the man of steel, 1980s style, would be considerably softer. His creators plan to make him "more vulnerable" and "more open about his feelings," and he will have "a more complicated relationship with Lois Lane." Jon, a male client describing this new development to us, laughed, then said seriously, "Men haven't had any motivation to change before now. Not in the fifties, that's for sure, and not during the sexual revolution, either. But now people want permanent relationships. They want to make things better for themselves—men want this just as much as women do. The trouble is, men don't know how. But at least now the *motivation* is there."

The motivation is there because, as Jon said, we can't go back to the fifties-style relationship, and the sexual revolution is a dinosaur. Meanwhile women, who no longer marry for financial security, are demanding more from men: more closeness, more equality, more intensity. Earlier in the book, we talked about Steve, who sensed within himself a terrible emptiness and a yearning to fill it. "But I have a classic case of cold feet," he said, half-jokingly. Several sessions later, he told us something about cold feet we'd never known. "Cold feet," it turns out, is actually a term in mountain climbing jargon for the physiological sensation a climber experiences when he is close to reaching his object of desire—the peak. Within striking distance, he will suffer sudden, extreme cold in the hands and feet, as well as a madly racing heart. What has been triggered all at once is the climber's *desire* to merge with the object—and his *fear* of merging with it. In their relationships with today's women, men are mountain climbers. A woman who embodies the possibility of an intimate relationship is the object of desire; at the same time, she is perceived as dangerous: if a man achieves closeness with her, he may be engulfed, or suffer a psychic loss of self that is equivalent to hurtling off the mountain into a dark chasm.

If, however, he arrives at the peak, he finds that it is exhilarating and fulfilling—still frightening, still a struggle, but not overwhelming, and well worth the work. "Nothing else really adds up," says Jon. "You can go to just so many bashes, so many clubs, see so many women, and work just so many hours a week. Then you look in the mirror one day and ask yourself what you're doing with your life. Not a helluva lot, you answer, if you're honest. But now, after I've been traveling for work and I come home to my wife and daughter, I'm ecstatic. I'm *human*. God knows it's been a struggle, and sometimes I think it should all be a lot easier. Okay, my relationship with Katherine isn't easy—but the struggle is worth it."

Eternal domestic bliss is a myth. But even if intimacy makes a man's heart race with fear and his limbs go numb with cold, the potential for both of you is more exciting than it's ever been before. Women shouldn't settle for less—nor should men.

Bibliography

We have selected the following books for those readers who would like to pursue new ideas that bear on men's intimacy problems, address the differences between men and women in their development and capacity for intimacy, and/or present a cultural context for male/female behavior.

CAPLAN, PAULA. *The Myth of Women's Masochism.* New York: E.P. Dutton, 1985.

CHODOROW, NANCY. *The Reproduction of Mothering: Psychoanalysis and the Sociology of Gender.* Berkeley: University of California Press, 1978.

DINNERSTEIN, DOROTHY. *The Mermaid and the Minotaur: Sexual Arrangements and Human Malaise.* New York: Harper & Row, 1976.

EHRENRICH, BARBARA. *The Hearts of Men: American Dreams and the Flight from Commitment.* New York: Anchor Press, 1983.

GILLIGAN, CAROL. *In a Different Voice: Psychological Theory and Women's Development.* Cambridge, Mass.: Harvard University Press, 1982.

Bibliography

LERNER, HARRIET GOLDHOR. *The Dance of Anger: A Women's Guide to Changing the Patterns of Intimate Relationships.* New York: Harper & Row, 1985.

LEVINE, LINDA and BARBACH, LONNIE. *The Intimate Male: Candid Discussions About Women, Sex and Relationships.* New York: New American Library, 1983.

PERSON, ETHEL, S. "The Omni-Available Woman and Lesbian Sex: Two Fantasy Themes and Their Relationship to the Male Developmental Experience." In *The Psychology of Men: New Psychoanalytic Perspectives,* edited by Gerald I. Fogel, Frederick M. Lane, and Robert S. Liebert. New York: Basic Books, 1986.

RUBIN, LILLIAN B. *Intimate Strangers: Men and Women Together.* New York: Harper & Row, 1983.

ABOUT THE AUTHORS

Dr. Sonya Rhodes is a psycotherapist in New York City specializing in couple and family therapy. She is on the faculty of the Postgraduate Center for Mental Health and is a consultant at the Jewish Board of Family and Children's Services. She earned her doctoral degree at Columbia University and has written extensively for professional journals. She is the senior author of *Surviving Family Life: The Seven Stages of Living Together.* Dr. Rhodes lectures at seminars and workshops around the country. She has been married for twenty-four years and has two teen-aged children.

Dr. Marlin S. Potash is a practicing psychotherapist and organizational consultant in New York City. She has been on the faculty of Harvard, Fordham, and Boston universities. Dr. Potash has written numerous articles on subjects including stress management, family relationships, and partnerships. She graduated from Tufts University and received her doctoral degree from Boston University. She is married and the mother of two preschool-aged daughters.